One of the Fifteen Million

NICHOLAS PRYCHODKO

One of the
Fifteen Million

LITTLE, BROWN AND COMPANY · BOSTON

AN UNCOMMON VALOR REPRINT EDITION
Complete and Unabridged

Printed in the United States of America

ISBN: 979-8-8691-6669-2

DEDICATION

*To the memory of my murdered father
and those ill-fated Ukrainians who lie
in countless obscure graves in Siberia.*

". . . It is obvious that it is you who is the professional writer. Your story moves along at a fast and absorbing pace, without distracting digression, and your descriptions are very vivid and illuminating without becoming tedious. With the current wave of trials in the Soviet Satellite countries, your personal account of Soviet penal and 'legal' methods should find a wide and interested audience."

LT. GEN. WALTER BEDELL SMITH

Former U.S.A. Ambassador to the U.S.S.R.

Foreword

"THERE is the man who has been in Hell!" whispered the common folk of Ravenna, as Dante Alighieri, author of the *Inferno*, strode sombrely along their streets. Canadians may far more truly say this of Nicholas Prychodko, a former junior professor in the University of Kiev, who was sent without trial in 1939 to spend several years at hard labour in the Soviet slave-camps of Siberia. He had previously been tortured for twenty-one months in a Soviet jail. His only offence had been that of thinking free thoughts in a slave state.

Canadians have far too long been deluded by the pro-Soviet propaganda of Communist traitors and even by Pro-Soviet rhapsodies purred from the pulpits of weak-minded fellow-travellers. It is time that the lid should be taken off the Pit of Leninist-Stalinist horror and that the smoke of Stalin's abominations should choke the lying throats of his prophets among us. Professor Prychodko writes out of personal experience of Communist iniquity. He bears on his body the scars of its cruelty. This is a terrible book, but it is the truth that is terrible and it must be faced, for the martyrdom of human freedom in the USSR is a martyrdom that the geopolitical planners in the Kremlin intend for us as well. Russian slave-camps for Canadians in Canada, manned by Russian police, are the objective of Stalin and his power-hungry agents among us. Every horror described in this book will be duplicated on Canadian soil if Communist plans prevail.

WATSON KIRKCONNELL
President of Acadia University

Preface

During the reign of the Czars a huge, three-storey prison was built on Shevchenko Boulevard, one of the busiest streets in Kiev. It was the third largest prison in Kiev and seemed to serve as a sort of warning from Moscow to the residents of the Ukrainian capital, purposely built in a crowded section. Its drab grey façade, with heavy bars over the windows, stretched for about five hundred feet along the boulevard.

Night and day two guards with fixed bayonets paced up and down in front of this massive building. From time to time the pale, tired faces of inmates peered out through the bars.

Twenty years later, before the outbreak of one of the worst Soviet purges and waves of terror, the "Yeshov terror" of 1937–1938, the political prisoners of the Communist régime were all taken out of this prison. The bars were removed and through the large, freshly-cleaned windows one could see a neat row of dining-tables, each covered with a white cloth and decorated with a bouquet of artificial flowers. White curtains appeared on all the windows of the upper storeys and trucks were seen bringing in material for workshops to be set up in the inner courtyard.

When the renovation was completed, new prisoners were brought in, not political prisoners, but men who were serving short-term sentences for minor crimes. They spent their time at constructive work in the workshops.

This show prison, on Shevchenko Boulevard in Kiev, was shown to foreign delegates and other visitors to convince them of Russia's "great humanitarianism."

From this prison it was only ten minutes' ride to the real Soviet prison where I was held for twenty-one months. From there I was taken away to slave labour in a Siberian concentration camp. In this book I shall endeavour to present to readers on the American continent a kaleidoscopic view of my experiences and impressions during that period of terror and injustice which still prevails behind the Iron Curtain.

NICHOLAS PRYCHODKO

Contents

One of the Fifteen Million

CHAPTER 1

Alarm

THE CITY OF KIEV, Capital of the Ukraine, was shrouded in a veil of ominous foreboding. Throughout that metropolis, and through the whole of the Ukraine, swept a merciless wave of terror. Each day, groups of people nervously approached the factory bulletin boards to scan the long lists of laid-off workmen. Each one expected to find his or her name on a list. Today, perhaps, there was no such name. But there remained the incessant fear that it would be there tomorrow.

And that would be the end. Relieved of work today and snatched away tomorrow, in the black of the night. Or perhaps they would come tonight, and the name would appear tomorrow. There was no avenue of escape, for the NKVD was omnipresent and its sleepless eye saw everything, everybody, everywhere.

Life was unreal and terrible. Christianity had disappeared from the minds of the oppressors who had seized power.

In the streets the threat of death became more menacing. With the approach of the evening when people left their work for their homes, and continued until dawn when they returned to their jobs. For people were everywhere allowed to proceed, apparently without hindrance, by the silent but all-seeing "Black Crows." These secret scourges pursued their course on the main street which leads from the Lukianiwska Prison to the Central and Regional Headquarters of the NKVD. In the dead of night they can be seen on the Great Vasylkivska Avenue on their way to Kossy Kapanir, an old Czarist fortress where soldiers awaiting court-martial were held, under the old regime. Its thick walls completely deaden the reports of the incessant shots in the nape of the victim's neck which are the order of the day there now.

From Kossy Kapanir it is not far to the Mysholovka ravines where it is easy to conceal any evidence of foul play and the bloody corpses of the citizens of this "happiest country on earth."

There was no peace, either on the street or at home. In the middle of the night one woke up trembling, chilled by the screech of the siren or the grating of suddenly opened entrance doors, holding one's breath, intently listening for the direction of the footsteps. And in the morning terrorized neighbours haltingly related the incident and whisper about who was taken away.

It was difficult to name a single dwelling place in Kiev where there had not been an arrest. Not only in Kiev, but throughout the whole Ukraine, from the largest cities to the most remote villages, the Kremlin's emissaries in their cranberry-red and blue caps, faithful stooges of Stalin and his "beloved *Narkom*" Yezhov, carried on their work of ferreting out victims. Periodic terrorization had ensued of all those who believed in freedom of thought and speech and who might become potential enemies. Especially was this true within the spheres of their "defensive interest" in Finland, or their interest in the "liberation" of the West Ukraine and Poland. All those who might have introduced a suggestion of discord or implied the slightest suspicion of the Kremlin had to be removed. At the same time millions of serfs had to be recruited for the slave camps at Kolyma and in Siberia.

CHAPTER 2

Nightmare

ONE NIGHT I had a dream. I was returning home only to find that the building in which I lived was no longer there. In its place was a massive stone structure with small grated windows. I opened the door, reinforced with iron braces, and entered. In the corridor there came from behind the multiple doors what seemed to be a subdued groan and commotion. I went in, listening all the while for the voice of my son, but I did not hear it. I came to the middle of the corridor and from behind one of the doors there came the sound of a familiar voice. I listened apprehensively. I clearly saw a number written in white over the door. I hurled myself against this door but it would not give. In the meantime some person holding a shotgun poked me in the back with the gun-stock. The door finally flew open from the impact of my body and I fell on a pile of leper-like people dressed in dirty tattered garments, agonizing in the last throes of death. With feverish speed and despair I sought but did not find my own child. It seemed as if I saw a hand extruding itself from this tangled mass of human flesh. I tried to rush forward but found myself rooted to the spot. I wanted to cry out but my voice failed me. Suddenly the door closed. I began to feel feverish. Beads of perspiration formed on my face.

I spent a sleepless night. A feeling of imminent doom seized my soul. In the morning I embraced my little son with more tenderness than usual. I felt something terrible and foreboding hovering about me although I was not one to indulge in mysticism. The next night my dream became a reality.

It was long past midnight. I woke with a start and sat up in bed. I listened intently. The sound of distant footsteps, coming closer and closer, reached my ears. The veins in my temples began to throb more and more violently as the steps drew nearer.

They stopped near my doorway. There was a short pause. Perhaps they were looking for the bell. Then there was a ring. Strangely, a load seemed to fall from my soul. The unbearable tension of constant anticipation lessened.

I calmly asked, "Who's there?"

"This is I, the janitor — for examination of passports."

Now I had not the slightest doubt. The janitor entered the room somewhat reluctantly, accompanied by two men in NKVD uniforms. One of them asked me with

simulated politeness to produce my passport. After examining it he ordered me to be searched.

My wife, evidently perplexed, began to dress, meanwhile consoling our sobbing son who was awakened by
the entrance of these strange men in uniform. Presently
I regained some semblance of self-control, and when they
began to search me I was on the look-out for any sur-
reptitious planting of false evidence, such as proclama-
tions or fire-arms. This was a routine device practised
quite extensively by the Yezhov "heroes." Their search
lasted over two hours, although our home contained only
one little room which served as dining-room, bedroom,
kitchen and study.

I recollect that the attention of one of these NKVD
men was drawn to a bottle of wine which he found
on a shelf. He kept turning it around in his hands against
the light so long that I finally suggested that they take
some. This they did, guzzling down the contents to
the very bottom. They then gathered up all the correspondence and papers they could find and told me
to get dressed, issuing no order for arrest in the meantime.

"Come with us; we wish to ask you for some explana-
tions."

When my wife asked them excitedly where they were
taking me, one of them answered, "Don't worry. I hope
this is a misunderstanding."

This was the stock answer everywhere, although the
"misunderstanding" usually ended with either a bullet

in the back of the head or years of imprisonment in a slave camp.

I did not as yet look for such a fate, and these words bolstered up the hope that this really might be a misunderstanding. For did not the newspapers continually assure us that the NKVD would not punish anybody unjustly? And was I not innocent of the smallest offence?

I dressed, meanwhile trying to calm my wife. After bidding her farewell and passionately embracing my son, I departed with my guards.

In the auto one of the guards sat next to me, watching my every move. Our conversation took on a different tone when I asked where they were taking me.

My suspicious fellow-passenger, who evidently had no desire to talk, merely blurted, "You will see."

In twenty minutes we arrived at the NKVD headquarters on Rosa Luxembourg Street and I was hustled inside.

One of my guards ordered me to go ahead. He opened the door and shoved me unceremoniously inside. We ascended a flight of stairs and then entered a large room. There I saw about two hundred people sitting on benches with their backs turned to the door, staring vacantly at the bare wall without once turning round, as if some strange purpose glued their vision to the spot. Three guards with pistols stood close by.

Noticing how interested I was in this peculiar scene, my guide opened a door in front of me with the laconic remark, "Do not look to the left."

There was a table in each corner of the room. Behind each table sat an indifferent and casual-looking NKVD official. My guide led me to one of the tables. Before the other tables stood men brought there probably under circumstances similar to my own. The official took the papers found in my apartment and subjected me to a few formal questions, jotting down the answers. When he was finished, I asked him for the return of an unfinished manuscript he had among my papers. I begged for its return so that I could complete it. Instead of handing it back to me he turned to his colleague at the next table with a derisive smirk.

"Did you hear that, Misha? This character wants to write a book!"

Misha looked me over and then burst into a hilarious guffaw.

With mock seriousness he said, "You're a writer? That's wonderful. You'll have an opportunity to write under the dictation of a fine professor."

The two officials and my guide let out a forced laugh at this sally. I was grasped roughly by the shoulder and shown the door. I was then literally thrust into the detention room and dumped among the rows of people facing the opposite wall. I was admonished gruffly not to turn around or engage in any conversation. The situation of the people sitting next to me was now quite evident.

The banter over my writing depressed and disheartened me; and now I too, like my companions on the bench, assumed the same hopeless stare into the emptiness of the wall, sitting it out with a sort of bovine patience.

Soon they began to lead us outside in groups where we were loaded on open trucks and driven off swiftly into the heavy grey fog of the early dawn.

The street-cars were not yet running; but many bent, dirty, grey figures were already trudging the streets to work. They looked up apprehensively at our passing vehicle, and no doubt must have had a premonition similar to our own when we, only yesterday, had seen the same kind of vehicle go by.

CHAPTER 3

Detention

THE GATES OPENED and our truck backed up to the gates of the Reception Depot in the courtyard of the Lukianiwska Prison. Before the gate stood four guards armed with rifles, watching against any attempt at escape and shouting intermittently:

"*Daway*, two men at a time."

In a few minutes we found ourselves in one of the large chambers of the Reception Depot. There were already about fifty people present who had been brought in previously. These people bore no resemblance whatever to the "enemies of the people," such as we saw on the propaganda placards in the city. They were the ordinary type of intelligentsia, workmen and officials. I studied them and could not help but feel that these were not felons. They had the stamp of honesty and hard work on them. Still we viewed each other cautiously, wondering what sin each might be concealing from the others.

Any remarks that were made among us were uttered guardedly and with reluctance. None of us wanted to risk a dangerous acquaintanceship with some planted "enemy of the people" for this might compromise our position which, we felt, was due to some misunderstanding that could be satisfactorily explained and duly settled.

There were those who felt a little more buoyant, knowing full well that all this talk about "misunderstanding" was a mere blind. They appeared to be more interested in the wide variety of racy inscriptions on the walls than in their own jeopardy. In a prominent place could be seen this choice reminder: "HE WHO WAS NOT HERE WILL BE HERE YET: HE WHO WAS HERE WILL NOT FORGET." And alongside this there was another inscription, a quotation from Dante's *Inferno:* "ALL HOPE ABANDON, YE WHO ENTER!" Needless to say I did not like to accept the implication, since I still did not wish to part with the hope that there was a misunderstanding.

About thirty more persons were brought into the cell, after which they began to usher out groups of five into the corridor. Then my turn came. We were made to undress and extend our arms out and bend down three times. Our clothes were gathered up and searched. Meanwhile we had to stand in the nude for about fifteen or twenty minutes on the cement floor. All metal buttons were torn off the clothing and all laces pulled out of the shoes. We learned later that there had been a number of suicides committed by cutting veins with buttons sharpened on the hard cement floor or by hanging from beds with woven shoe-strings tied around the neck. After the search was over we were led into an office where prison records were completed and from there into another chamber. We wound our arms around our waists with embarrassment as if in sudden pain.

In the evening the doors opened and a group of railroad men from Fastov were driven into the cell. One glance was enough to suggest that some railroad catastrophe was the reason for their incarceration. Their faces were literally covered with black and blue marks and some bore signs of freshly inflicted bloody gashes. We all rushed forward to question them about the accident but they were reluctant to explain, no doubt because of their strange surroundings and for fear of causing provocation. But one of them finally became communicative.

"This catastrophe took place at the Fastov NKVD office during interrogation," he said.

We asked them such questions as: "Were you actually beaten while you were being questioned? How was that possible? We thought such a thing was only practised in capitalist countries!"

Of course not all of us were so naïve about it, but those who were became disillusioned when he said: "Impossible, you say; well, take a look at me! If and when you get a few clouts with a chair-leg you'll know different."

This episode had a depressing effect on the uninitiated, which was deepened by the memory of the brutal behaviour of the guards during the search, and by the fact that we had received neither food nor water during the whole day.

About one o'clock at night we were ordered outside into the inner court of the prison. By the light of the lanterns I saw the main façade of the prison. I remembered having seen an identical façade before; and then it suddenly dawned upon me. This was the prison I had dreamed about just prior to my arrest. It was unbelievable but true.

We were led across the yard to the washroom, where they cut off our hair. This operation was performed with unnecessary brutality by young degenerates from the criminal division. They abused us with the most vulgar and obscene epithets. We learned later that these same youngsters did the women-prisoners' hair-cuts as well. All our clothing was taken to be disinfected, and later returned in a badly scorched condition. They then turned on alternately hot and cold water for our bath. After this satisfaction they took us out into the yard at about three o'clock in the morning, keeping us there about an hour in the cold. Some one timidly tried to protest against this treatment but was rewarded with a resounding blow delivered by a guard.

An hour later the guards began to herd us in groups of twenty into the Prison. My group was taken up into one of the corridors on the second floor. We were halted at the end of this corridor and then marshalled in twos and threes into various cells. Another prisoner and I came to an iron-braced door which had a peep-hole in the centre and on which the number "109" was painted in white. My dream was again recalled.

The door opened and we entered. We could hear the grating of an iron bar behind us; and before us there appeared one of the most unbelievable sights that the most imaginative person enjoying freedom could conjure up. In this brilliantly lighted cell, about fifteen feet by twenty, fourteen iron cots were set up in tiers of threes, one on top of the other, reaching almost to the ceiling. On each of the cots four people were lying sideways, the end persons being tied to the cot with towels, to prevent them from falling off in their sleep.

Against the back wall there stood a long cupboard, a foot in depth, with shelves for dishes. On the top of it lay a man who assumed the proud demeanour of a king. He had, comparatively, so much more room than the others. The whole cement floor under the bunks was covered with human forms, packed like herrings in a barrel. All were lying on their sides and, as I was to learn afterwards, one could only turn over if everyone else was willing to turn at the same time. We had standing room only near the door and could not move, for fear of trampling on somebody's head. On our appearance many sleepy, dirty heads were raised; but seeing nothing out of the ordinary, were soon lowered again. The orderly told us to remain standing in the same position until morning.

Cursing the prison administration for letting more people into the cell, he said:

"What the devil are they thinking about; we already have one hundred and sixteen persons here!"

There was not only no freedom of movement in the cell, but one could hardly breathe, especially while standing up. The awful stench of human perspiration and of the barrel-like urinal took one's breath away. We had to bend down low in order to breathe at all. From time to time some sleepy looking scare-crow in human form would make his way from some part of the room to the urinal. This was extremely difficult as it had to be done over many closely packed bodies. Some of them took it with good grace; but others cursed or else dealt the "prowler" a blow. Those who passed by us stopped to ask questions such as where we came from; what was going on in the free outside world; whether there was any talk of an amnesty; and after they had completed their toilet they threaded their way over the protesting forms back to their places.

We did not ask them any questions for fear of annoying the inmates; but we observed much. If we had not found ourselves in the same fix, we would not only have regarded their plight with compassion, but it would have appeared comical as well. Later, when I was liberated, I often wished that I possessed a snapshot of this scene because mere words are inadequate to describe it.

On one of the top cots a large, black-bearded man was snoring vociferously. He looked like one of those fantastic highwaymen who had somehow managed to survive from the seventeenth or eighteenth century. But he turned out to be Professor B.I., one of the leading astronomers at the Kiev Observatory, a person of great learning and of a genial and optimistic nature. When I told him later, after making his acquaintance, that I mistook him for a mediaeval outlaw, he laughed heartily. He never lost his sense of humour. Even when he was being subjected to the third degree and forced to admit guilt as a mythical spy on the German pay-roll, Professor B.I., ostensibly unable to endure any further torture, wrote out a legendary confession, admitting to a series of systematic meetings with the German Schopenhauer in the library of the Ukrainian Academy of Sciences.

The young prosecutor, on hearing the name Schopenhauer, felt highly elated at being able to force these admissions, and with the exuberance of youth he hurried to his chief with the evidence and to ask for further instructions. But it was not long before he and the chief of the division returned in great anger.

"Do you think," yelled the officer, "that we are so stupid that we have never heard of Schopenhauer?"

Professor B.I. was given a vigorous beating for his fictitious confession.

Our observations were interrupted by a shrill ring in the corridor. Everybody rose swiftly from his place. The greatest speed was manifested by those occupying the top cots, since only fifteen minutes were allowed in which to take the cots apart and line up for inspection. There was considerable confusion in the cell since everybody inadvertently got in everybody else's way. Nevertheless the cots were disassembled and placed against the walls. The prisoners then formed into rows. Since all of them could not find room on the floor simultaneously, four rows had to stand on the cots. Soon there was a screech of the bar and the guard from the doorway ordered: "Attention!" Some degenerate, calling himself "over-seer of the corridor," entered the cell. He got up on the urinal to get a better view and with extended forefinger began to count us like a herd of cattle. He made an entry in a notebook and then silently and pompously made his exit.

When we began to fall out of line again, we were so crowded that we found it difficult to pass one another. The new arrivals were questioned about events in the free world and whether there was any talk of amnesty. Of course we had heard nothing in respect to that — it was just a pious hope of the prisoners. On the contrary we could only tell them that the number of arrests was growing and that the people's morale was getting worse.

On the other hand, we were interested in the conditions of prison incarceration, in the methods of examination and in the charges. What we were told dissipated any optimism in this regard. The questioning was followed up with merciless beatings; and then the prisoners were forced to admit to fictitious crimes, or else they were made to sign confessions that were cooked up by the prosecution itself. We had no further doubts about this spurious and forced information, especially when two of our new acquaintances bared their backs and showed how the flesh was streaked with horrible black marks.

CHAPTER 4

An Enemy of the People

I RATHER UNEXPECTEDLY met one of my old acquaintances in the cell — Professor L., formerly a district school inspector in Kiev. I had heard before that he had been arrested as an "enemy of the people," and this had seemed somewhat strange to me. He had always appeared to be a modest and hard-working sort of person and it was hard to conceive him guilty of any crime or subversive action. But when he was arrested I began to wonder whether there really was something wrong, for surely the NKVD would not do this to an innocent man! The more the terror raged, the greater grew the propagandistic eulogies about the justice of Soviet jurisprudence.

This man finally came over to me and shook hands. If he had not told me his name I would not have recognized him. It was hard to believe that this was the same person, so greatly had he changed in the two months since his arrest. His features were heavily furrowed and tired-looking and his face was covered with a thick stubble. The right eye was completely closed by a reddish-blue swelling.

"What happened to you?" I asked.

He replied, "I think you ought to have some inkling of what is going on by now. I don't know why they arrested me, and yet I have been questioned six times already. The day before yesterday I received these mementoes for refusing to sign a false statement. Look at my eye; but don't think that is all," he said, pulling up his shirt with trembling hands to disclose the black and blue welts on his chest and spine.

"What happened to you?" I asked with horror and on the verge of tears.

"My prosecutor," he continued, "has an oak board armed with the points of twenty nails. While he is questioning me he makes me take off my shirt and he conducts his investigation with the aid of this instrument. I can't stand much more of this. Perhaps I'll have to give in and confess to something."

It gradually became clear to me that these people were no more "enemies of the people" than I was; but as yet I could not see any sense in this mass persecution of wholly innocent people. It was not until later on in my prison term that it all became obvious, especially when I encountered a group being sent to the dark and limitless forests of Siberia. There was wealth in those forests in the form of foreign exchange. But who would want to go there of his own free will, to freeze in the intense cold, or feed with his blood the myriads of mosquitoes at the price of a crust of bread and a pint of sloppy soup made from decayed fish? In those parts millions of men were needed. That explained the double purpose they had in mind: first, to forestall any danger of rebellion among the people who might get ideas about the hypocrisy of the Stalin Constitution and expose the humbug to others; and secondly, to secure cheap slave labour which could be utilized without cost even within the Arctic Circle. There they can squeeze the last ounce of energy out of the prisoners and then bury them without leaving any trace in the silence of the inaccessible *taiga.*

And why the interrogations, the false evidence and the trumped-up charges? This was all to justify the existence of the millions of loyal brutes comprising the NKVD. And then there was the propaganda aspect, as much as to say: "You see how the sleepless eye of the NKVD is guarding your welfare. You are hungry and without clothes because of these wreckers and diversionists. Read for yourself their own admissions."

I well remember them reading out the fantastic evidence of one of my fellow-workers at one of the meetings, touching on his alleged sabotage and spying activities.

Insulted and enraged, somebody shouted, "Well! Who would have thought that such a type could be so deceiving? The NKVD is really on the job; it sees and knows everything."

But when I saw the bloody welts on Professor L.'s

spine I knew how and under what circumstances this "evidence" was signed and secured.

Professor L. incidentally asked me whether I had heard anything about his family and whether the relations of those arrested were being molested. I answered him in the negative, since I did not wish to worry him unduly with recitals of cases I had known of where the wives of arrested persons were asked publicly to renounce their husbands as "enemies of the people." This request was usually accompanied by a flourish of the false evidence. There were some women, dumbfounded by these "crimes" and the terrifying "secret subversiveness" of their husbands, who signed such renouncements and then published them in the newspapers, or else publicly announced them at the meetings of the institutions where their husbands had been employed. And thus it happened that the public at large, reading these renunciations, came to believe in the truth of the accusations. But not all wives did this.

The penalty for the least hesitation or shadow of doubt on the part of relatives was either imprisonment or else banishment from Kiev to some provincial town under continual surveillance of the NKVD.

The prison inmates were ignorant of these facts because of their isolation. And as for correspondence and personal contact with relatives — that was simply out of the question! The most that relatives could do was to send fifty rubles a month to a prisoner, so that he might buy himself some essentials.

This money was received by the prison administration and deposited in the prisoner's account. On very rare occasions he was allowed to buy a loaf of black bread, some *makhorka*, or an onion, which were peddled along the corridors. The price of these was deducted from his account. For the smallest offence, such as an audible whisper by one of the inmates, everyone in the cell was deprived of the privilege of buying these things. If this money was returned to the sender it meant that the prisoner was no longer there, but no information was ever given as to his or her whereabouts.

Every morning at dawn the lights in the cell were put out and we were left in the shadows, as in a cellar; for the windows of the cell were enclosed by diagonally-set iron shutters. Thus nothing could be seen of the outside world, from which only a thin ray of light filtered in. There was method in this madness: to isolate the inmates from the rest of the prison and to impress upon them the unpleasant understanding: "You 'enemies of the people' might as well know that you are worse than dogs."

This semi-darkness was, of course, intended to depress the inmates and to break morale. Conversation was allowed only in whispers. The punishment for conversation in an ordinary tone of voice was the *kartser*; or else the offender was taken out into the corridor by the guard, who "explained" the regulation with the aid of a four-pound bar from the door. Underlying all this bestial persecution was the obvious plan to degrade the dignity of the prisoners; to harass them morally and physically; as well as to soften them up and thus lighten the burden of the investigator.

The deadly monotony of prison life was a further addition to the wretchedness of the inmates. In the morning — a check-up; an hour later — opening of the doors. Then the doling out of bread, "coffee" with a little sugar, and some sort of stinking liquid that the prisoners called *balanda*. In the evening all we were given was a drink of the same "coffee" made of a rejected grade of barley. During the whole time of our incarceration we suffered from perpetual and gnawing hunger.

Strange as it may seem, the fifteen minutes we were allowed for toilet purposes were the only bright moments in our bleak and dreary prison existence. The toilet room was the only place where we could pick up bits of information which might help to break the terrible monotony. The prisoners from every cell took advantage of this retreat to find out what newly incarcerated prisoners in the other cells had to say about the outside world. This news was frequently scratched on the wall with a sharpened match stem; and it took very close scrutiny to decipher the message. News was also transferred by means of cigarette papers, hidden behind a dislodged brick or a water pipe.

Notwithstanding the most diligent searches each cell managed somehow to salvage a tiny bit of lead pencil which the inmates guarded like a great treasure. And although the guards carefully scrutinized the toilet-room after we left, this "central post office" kept right on functioning. Even a three to five day confinement of the writers in the *kartser* by the guards who spotted them through a peep-hole in the door failed to stop the messages.

Another pleasant break was our fresh-air walk; but it lasted only ten minutes. The inmates of each cell in turn were led across the corridor into the inner court, an asphalted circle ninety-five paces in circumference around which we promenaded in pairs, with our hands behind our backs. We were not allowed to look either up or around, even though nothing could be seen but walls and shuttered windows. Punishment for any infraction of this rule was a vigorous blow and the offender had to stand against the wall at attention.

Two chestnut trees that used to grow luxuriantly in the centre of the court were cut down so as to deprive the prisoners of any pleasanter scenery than the dirty drabness of their cells.

On one of the walls of the promenade court, bolted to a ledge, was a painted box with the inscription: "Box for complaints to the *Narkom* Yezhov of the NKVD USSR." This box, of course, was not intended for the inspection of visitors. As far as the prisoners were concerned it was meant as an act of mockery. How could they write complaints when the mere possession of a pencil or a piece of paper was an offence? And to whom were they to write? To the satrap of Stalin who had

caused millions of innocent people to be shot and murdered?

Nevertheless this box did serve us later on as a source
of news. One day, when we were out for our walk, we
did not see the box in its usual place. This meant that
Yezhov was no longer in power. The current wave of
terrible and indiscriminate terror was receding. Two days
later the box was back again; but this time there was a
notice that complaints would be received in the name of
Narkom Beria. This confirmed our suspicions in regard
to Yezhov.

CHAPTER 5

The Discipline of Fear

ON MY VERY FIRST DAY in prison I made the acquaintance of "H.S.," a student in the fourth year in Kiev University's language and literature faculty. He sat opposite me not far from the door; for since he had arrived only four days before he did not have any pretensions to a "grandstand seat," as it were, in a quieter corner. He also had a three-year-old son. In the dead of night a car had driven up to his place, as to mine. He was searched and then driven off to the prison department of the NKVD on Rosa Luxembourg Street. There he was led down into a deep windowless cellar and stood up against a wall. Four men with rifles faced him. He did not know what it was all about; and at times he thought this must be only a terrible nightmare. When he timidly tried to ask the guards the reason for all this procedure they merely stared at him in stony silence.

After a lapse of about fifteen or twenty minutes a man in the uniform of an NKVD officer entered, holding a paper in his hands. Unfolding it he began to read: "By authority of the NKVD resolved, that the student H.S. belonged to a subversive, Ukrainian nationalist, terrorist organization, aiming at the destruction of the existing order and planning terrorist action against leading members of the party and the government; therefore by virtue of the Ukrainian Criminal Code, Article 54, the NKVD USSR College sentences him to the highest penalty of the social law: Death. This verdict is to be executed immediately."

The person who read the verdict gave a command, and four dim barrels were levelled at H.S. Beads of perspiration burst out on the forehead of the youngster. H.S. fell on his knees and extended his arms pleadingly towards the man who had read the verdict.

"This is a strange mistake — my name is H.S., but I never heard of such an organization."

The person in uniform interrupted him sternly. "Don't be an idiot; we know everything; you can save your life only by a complete and honest confession. You are duty-bound to disclose the names of your fellow-conspirators."

And then the person in uniform, having ordered the guards to lower the gun-barrels, handed H.S. another paper on which was written: "I, H.S., executive member of a Ukrainian, nationalist, terrorist organization, hereby acknowledge that our organization, has as its aim . . . and furthermore . . . that the following persons were active members thereof." A long list of friends and personally known students was appended.

H.S. tried desperately to convince them that he was

ignorant of any such organization; but in answer the gun-barrels were raised again and H.S. signed the "evidence." He was then led to our cell.

Life now became purgatory to H.S. He tried to console himself with the illusion that this was all a mistake, and that the NKVD could not conceivably lend itself to such a frame-up of false evidence. He did not know until later that this is the usual Russian police trick of trying to find out the psychological reaction of all newly brought in and uninformed prisoners.

About two weeks later he was taken in for questioning again, and after being unmercifully tortured he was compelled to acknowledge the "truth" of the evidence signed by him in the presence of the persons on the list. H.S. always returned to the cell filled with despair and remorse. Lacking character and strength of will, however, he continued to sign the fantastic statements against himself and others, in spite of the fact there was no truth in them.

This case ended in the conviction of the whole "organization." The prisoners were sentenced to ten years at slave labour in Siberia. These "preventive" measures were carried out against an imaginary menace with utter disregard for the lives of thirty-two young men which were broken forever.

The powerful and exorbitantly paid NKVD Organization had to do something to justify its existence. It therefore fabricated on paper countless fantastic organizations seeking to bring about a change in government or allegedly guilty of disruptive action. Stooping even to murder to get the "evidence" was not unusual.

The *seksots* of the NKVD were scattered everywhere, in every strata of the population. They recorded every word and every sign of dissatisfaction. These crimes were described with all the cunning nuances of the devious, cruel and despicable police mind; and subordinate officials had to originate and coordinate the activities of bogus "counter-revolutionary organizations" throughout the whole of the USSR. To this end victims were ferreted out everywhere.

Of course most people in the USSR are quite aware of all this; but fear makes them tongue-tied. Everybody is afraid to exchange confidences even with his best friend. The NKVD system of internal espionage among citizens of the "free and liberty-loving" USSR has been developed to an incredible degree. Mass underground organization in Russia is impossible — not that the population loves the regime, for three quarters of the people regard it with revulsion — but because in the highly organized system of Soviet espionage and mutual distrust, mass revolt would be out of the question. In view of this, how naïve was the American who made the observation to me: "You say that the majority of the people are against Stalin? That's a lie! If that were the case he would not have been chosen as the leader of the nation."

The information of the *seksot* in the USSR does not have to be corroborated by facts and investigation. Our numerous prison experiences convinced us of this. Some of the former NKVD officials incarcerated along with us in the cells admitted that this was the case.

Another fellow-prisoner, S. Kabeka, was a railway conductor. His regular run had been between Shepetivka and Zdolbunovo, on the Polish boundary. He lived near a half-way station, midway between those two points. According to the regulations of the border officials he, as well as others, had no right to get off the train at the mid-way station on the return journey from Poland. He could only return home after having stayed over at Shepetivka.

Once when Kabeka had a day off and was at home, he was visited by his brother-in-law, who came from Zdol-bunovo. This man brought with him a bottle of Polish cognac and some lunch, and the family spent the evening in pleasant conversation. In the course of the conversa-tion the brother-in-law made the casual remark that the people in Poland lived better than the people in the USSR.

The next day Kabeka, who was not only a conductor but also a *seksot*, sent the following information to the NKVD:

"On Friday, having broken the regulations of the bor-der officials, on the way from Zdolbunovo, came M.D. to S. Kabeka. He brought illegally with him a bottle of Polish cognac. (I do not know where he got it.) After he had a few drinks, he began to tell about how much better the people in Poland live than those in the USSR, enumerating certain facts. Kabeka helped sustain the conversation." To this information against his brother-in-law was signed his signature under his *seksot* pseudonym.

This information went its devious way and lay idle until the year 1938, when M.D. as well as Kabeka himself were arrested. This man Kabeka happened to be incarcerated in our cell.

After a few days Kabeka was called out for questioning. He was unmercifully beaten in order to force him to sign a confession of espionage on behalf of Poland. This "treatment" was repeated again and again.

At first Kabeka was able to come back to the cell by himself. Later he was dragged along the corridor and thrown in half-dead. Kabeka refused to admit any guilt, but he had already reached the point where the cruel torture was getting too much for him. In a day or so he would not be able to resist signing the usual specious confession. And when that day finally came, he was subjected to the following by the investigator.

"So you don't want to sign? What do you think you are? A saint? Do you forget the anti-Soviet conversation you had favouring Poland at your home with M.D. when he came to visit you with a bottle of cognac? You think we don't know anything; but we know everything! I helped you, and now you had better write what happened before and after this. Do not conceal anything, for we already know every move you have made."

Kabeka now realized what he was up against, but he still tried passionately to convince the investigator that neither before nor after the conversation did he have anything to do with espionage; and that he always had been a conscientious *seksot;* also that the information about his brother-in-law was written by himself under his own pseudonym. The investigator listened throughout and then told him again that the NKVD knew everything and so could not be bamboozled. He then let Kabeka go back to his cell.

Although Kabeka had been severely maltreated, his disposition now began to improve noticeably. He said his case was one of mistaken identity and that was why he was beaten and that he had never in any way been mixed up in such an affair.

For over three months he was not called out again for questioning. He kept waiting from day to day for his release; and during the whole time he became more reticent in his relations with us.

And then one day he was called out, but without his belongings. He returned fifteen minutes later on the verge of hysteria. At first he maintained a rigid silence but finally he opened up and admitted receiving a ten-year sentence by the OSO. Kabeka was enraged at this "injustice"; and so out of pure pique, confided the details of his case to a friend.

To tell the truth, we would have signed our own signatures to this verdict, for in his former capacity Kabeka must have sent many innocent persons to a much worse fate.

Near my place in the cell sat a forty-year-old man, apparently a peasant. What drew my attention to him was the complete lack of worry on his features. He spoke about all the prison affairs, tragic though they were, humorously and in unrestrained fashion. Many were the pointed barbs he threw in the direction of the prison administration and the investigators. He was gifted with both wit and natural common sense, a teller of tall tales, a type not unusual in any Ukrainian village. In his case however, these tales were flavoured with political satire, a thing not approved by the local police authorities who henceforth kept the story-teller under surveillance.

And here is how my new peasant friend, K. from Boyarka near Kiev, happened to be in jail. He had been sitting one evening in the village co-operative store relating the following story.

"Yesterday evening I was returning from a neighbouring village when suddenly a wolf jumped out from a bush. I yelled at him, stamped my feet, and he ran back into the forest. I sped with all haste in order to avoid any misfortune. But my path was blocked by three more. I began to yell again as hard as I could, scaring them back into the woods, and then I fled. I had hardly gotten out of the forest when I was met by a whole pack of wolves. I propped my back up against a tree, gathered up some brush around me and started a fire. The wolves surrounded me, bared their fangs and kept creeping closer and closer, unmindful of the burning twigs I was throwing at them. They looked very ferocious and hungry. I was afraid to leave the fire and get more brush. Meanwhile the blaze had gone down, and I saw imminent death approaching me. But then an ingenious thought occurred to me. I grabbed my notebook and pencil and yelled:

" 'If you're going to be like that, I'm going to allocate you to the *Kolkhoz!*'

"When I said this, those wolves vanished instantly. I then filled my pipe and lighted it, wiped the perspiration off my face and went home."

For this the story-teller got the usual beating and five years in Siberia as well.

I remember how, when he was informed from the corridor about this verdict, he poked his head through the doorway of the cell, saying, "Thank you, Comrade Stalin, for not forgetting me even in prison."

CHAPTER 6

A Pedlar with a Grindstone

TWO DAYS LATER our cell had another occupant. A beggar in appearance, he did not seem at all downcast. On the contrary, he seemed rather glad to have found a place to stay. When the guard opened the door of the cell to let him in, the beggar turned around at the threshold and asked somewhat irritably:

"And where is my grindstone?"

"You will get it in the next world along with the charcoal," answered the guard, as he slammed the door behind him.

The new prisoner merely thumbed his nose at the retreating figure and then greeted the inmates of the cell.

"The best of health, fellows!"

He made himself at home in the cell immediately.

"I don't give a damn for being brought here; but the sons of bitches not only didn't give me a snort, they took my grindstone away."

He spoke up boldly, disregarding the warning that such talk was dangerous. We asked him how he had been picked up and he immediately told us his story.

"I was going along the Great Pidvalny Street with my grindstone on my way to Sinbaz. As I passed the German Consulate a door opened and a young woman called me in. I entered and she led me into a kitchen where she handed me some knives, scissors and other articles to sharpen. Naturally I sharpened them. She paid me twenty rubles and ushered me out. I went along in a good humour, deciding that I would buy a hundred grams of garlic sausage and some vodka to feast on.

"I had hardly reached Stolypin Street when I was accosted by two plainclothes men.

" 'Come with us,' they said.

" 'Where?' I asked.

" 'You'll know,' they answered.

"They led me across the street and shoved me into a car; but they did not want to take the grindstone along. I protested, telling them that I would not go without my grindstone. They did not want to create a disturbance; so they threw the grindstone down at my feet, and then drove on. They brought me directly to this place, recorded my case at their office, left my grindstone in the corridor and even took my money. And now will some one give me a smoke?" Some one gladly accommodated him with some *makhorka*, and he subsided somewhat.

"Has anyone here got a swig of something?" he asked.

On receiving a negative reply he rent the atmosphere with curses. His greatest source of dissatisfaction was his inability to find a drink; and his red nose showed sufficient evidence of intimate acquaintanceship with vodka.

At first he raged to the point of illness at his unaccustomed and "dry" confinement; but when he realized how hopeless were his chances of release, he began to cool down and acclimatize himself.

In another two weeks he was called for questioning again in regard to his alleged espionage on behalf of Germany. He was asked how long he was in communication with the Consulate and what were the services rendered. But since he was not at all guilty of any such crime, the investigation took on the form of "factual argumentation." And when at last he became convinced that this beating on his back with a chair-leg would never cease he finally decided to sign the bogus confession of espionage. This he did with a cross, being unable to write. Afterwards he managed to wheedle a package of cigarettes out of the investigator and seemed to find satisfaction in this act as a sort of revenge. But he was not successful in securing a drink of whisky.

He spent four months with us in our cell; and then he was led out to serve a ten-year sentence from the OSO, or to put it in his own words, "to seek new bread."

CHAPTER 7

Order of Merit

THE INMATES OF OUR CELL ranged from learned academicians to stupid beggars, from sublime characters to ridiculous buffoons. They were a polyglot conglomeration of nationalities: once we counted thirteen. But the Ukrainians were in the majority — a nation most "beloved by the older Muscovite brother." There were even high officials and military leaders. The Kremlin was always in constant dread of any person exerting real influence in military circles. Often the only reason for their arrest was the recitation of an anecdote or some picayune reference to government policy.

One day the commander of the Bila Tserkva Division was brought into our cell. He wore the Order of Lenin on his chest, the "Red Flag," and the "Red Star." It seemed strange they had not been ripped off before he entered the prison, but perhaps it was done with a view to impressing upon the prisoners the mighty reach of the penalizing hand.

At first the attitude of this commander was one of contemptuous haughtiness towards the other inmates. He evidently took the view, like ourselves earlier, that his arrest was just a misunderstanding, and that the other prisoners were actually "enemies of the people," such as he, not so long ago, had been denouncing in his speeches. He looked down his nose at us when we asked him questions.

In the evening of that same day he was taken out, along with his insignia, for questioning. He returned at dawn, or rather he was dragged back and thrown into the cell. He was splattered with blood, and the cloth where his insignia had been sewn was torn to shreds.

Choking with blood, which he kept spitting out, he found it hard to talk.

His wounds were washed, and he was laid down in a quiet corner on two coats which were spread out to make his rest easier.

When he came to after a short nap, he began to relate how the investigator, prior to the interrogation, rushed over to him and tore off the insignia, calling them "rattle-toys," and ripped his shirt to pieces. Unable to stand such degradation, this commander of a division who had won his awards on the Spanish front, threw caution to the winds, picked up a chair and knocked the investigator off his feet. Hearing his cry for help, some guards hurried in from the corridor and flung themselves at the prisoner. They all gave full vent to their natures with the help of oak chair-legs.

Forgotten were his services as an active commander in

their passion to give him "the works." When he fainted, they revived him again, and the torture was renewed.

Once more the same day, the commander was recalled for questioning, but he never returned to our cell again. Notwithstanding our efforts to find out more about him, we found no trace of his whereabouts or what was done with him.

In this manner prison life continued, the inmates slowly accustoming themselves to its hard and cruel routine. Human adaptability seems limitless; and in normal times the human mind can hardly conceive of the amount of pain and suffering it can endure.

There was little rest in the NKVD prison at night. The judicial investigation would begin about 11 P.M. and continue till 2 A.M. Some prisoners were interrogated, others simply disappeared. In such a strained atmosphere, sleep was out of the question except in snatches of fitful semi-consciousness. Whenever the door bar squeaked, everybody, as if electrified, lifted his head and waited. Into the prison cell would move a guard with a list of names and call, for instance:

"With K?"

Then all prisoners whose surname began with that letter had to give their names. When the surname was given, the Christian name was asked.

Then the order followed: "Dress quickly!"

Sometimes the fatal words "with belongings" were added. The victim would dress with trembling hands and walk out of the cell into the corridor; his fellow inmates bade their farewells in silence. Ten or twenty minutes later the door would open again and the guard would ask for names beginning with some other letter. Thus four to six men from each cell would be called. The torture chamber was working at full speed. Hardly a night passed without such visits.

At daybreak or even later, some of the victims would return from the investigation room to our cell, their faces unrecognizable from wounds and bloodstains. Often the victim was no longer able to walk, so the guards would pull him by the legs or the arms along the prison corridors, and throw him into our cell as if he were an inanimate bundle. Some individuals would be called to the investigation room night after night for weeks in succession. These victims would drop into a coma or become insane after so many nights of sleeplessness and suffering. In such a stupefied frame of mind they would sign any imaginary statement fabricated by the investigator.

Some victims never came back. Whether they were tortured to death or shot in the nape of the neck we could not find out. On the following day the guard would come to our cell and take away the belongings of the victim who had not returned.

Practically every night there would be an additional horror-drama enacted — a shrill, unearthly female shriek would come from the investigation chambers where some woman was being tortured. The interrogation of women was often conducted at night in order to further demoralize the men. The investigation chambers were in the basement between the sixth and eleventh corridors.

In moments like these we would sink to the bottomless pit of despair. We would listen breathlessly, apprehensively. Perhaps we would hear the voice of a sister, a mother, a wife, or a daughter. Those who could not stand these shrieks soon became hysterical, giving vent to blood-curdling yells like the cries of a wounded beast. The person guilty of such yelling would soon be discovered, pulled out into the corridor, and silenced with kicks.

One scene still rises before me like a bad dream. An inmate of our cell, a Red Army major, committed suicide by striking his head with all his might against the sharp corner of a brick chimney. With blood gushing from the wound, he fell down unconscious. He was instantly removed from the cell. Later we found that he had died the same night.

Along the sixth corridor of the prison, special cells were allocated for those who had been condemned to die. Terrible cries of agony often emanated from them. They were frequently interrupted as if the victims were being gagged; then there would be one more redoubled yell that dwindled down to an inaudible gurgle.

In moments like these, we resembled the inmates of an insane asylum more than ordinary prisoners in a jail. It was not until these heart-rending cries had subsided that sleep of any kind was possible. Even what little snatches we did get were often broken by the shrill scream of a victim.

Under these conditions I pondered over my forthcoming interrogation, although I had committed no crime. It finally dawned on me that the guilt need not be genuine. It was all predetermined by Yezhov, who declared before a meeting of top NKVD officials in Kiev:

"What kind of NKVDists are you that you cannot produce confessions? So long as there is a man, a crime can be found!"

To the firm denial of a prisoner, the investigator would often reply with a repetition of these famous words:

"All the same you'll write. So long as there is a man, we will find the crime!"

And in most cases they did find the crime: by means of a chair leg, a rubber hose; by closing a door on the victim's fingers, by pumping air into the prisoner's stomach; and other Soviet investigation methods. Many of those who at first resolutely refused to sign ended up by doing so when they realized how hopeless their position was.

Such prisoners would usually return to their prison cells unharmed. In fact they would be rewarded by the investigator with two or three cigarettes for their legendary crimes. These individuals were spontaneously boycotted by the prisoners at large, despite the fact that open boycotts of a fellow-prisoner were strictly punished and were also dangerous because the boycotted inmate could revenge himself by provocation. But we all showed the deepest respect and sympathy towards those prisoners who steadfastly suffered persecution and refused to submit to giving false evidence.

One of the most remarkable figures I met in the prison was Mikhailo Savchuk, a member of the Ukrainian Academy of Sciences.

For sixteen successive nights he was led out for questioning and dreadfully beaten, because he refused to admit that a group of his colleagues were guilty of membership in a nationalist organization. The admission of this membership, imaginary, of course, was needed by the NKVD police to create a formal basis for the arrest of the other members of the Ukrainian Academy of Sciences.

Mikhailo Savchuk categorically refused to yield to this type of provocation, and consequently was tormented every night. At first he used to return from the torture chamber all alone and covered with bruises and bloodstains, pretending the while that everything was all right with him. Later on he could not walk at all, so the jailers threw him in like a sack on the floor of our cell. Even then he did not show any sign of pain except for an occasional shudder of agony.

Once I approached him, asking whether there was anything I could do for him. Actually, there was nothing I could do, yet I felt like saying some kind word to him. He understood and thanked me warmly.

"How can you stand all these tortures without losing your mental balance?" I asked him.

"I shall disclose to you," he said, "the secret of my tenacity. When they torture me, I imagine I see in the corner of the cell my sick wife standing there and holding my little daughter in her arms. Realizing fully the burden of their solitude and utter poverty, I feel it so keenly and so painfully that my physical suffering becomes less excruciating. I know that if I falsely sign the paper they demand, my loved ones will be bereft of their last shelter, and that none of my friends, who would take me then for a most contemptible wretch, would ever condescend to speak a kind word to them. Let me die in vain, but with a clear conscience. You follow my example and do likewise."

This conversation had a profound effect on me. My soul was greatly relieved. My friend's noble example strengthened me to endure all the tortures of which I, too, received my full share.

Three days after my conversation with Mikhailo Savchuk, he was dragged into the cell half dead.

We applied poultices to the sorest spots on his body and made room for him under a cot in the corner of our cell. He hardly moaned. We only heard him move from time to time from one wounded side to the other. Later we thought we heard him snore once rather noisily, perhaps in a nightmare. Then he was quiet. Everybody was glad that he was resting so nobody disturbed him. This time he slept longer than usual. We did not wake him up even when our jail dinner was brought in. But in the evening we decided to waken him. We called him by name, but he didn't move. We immediately understood that there was something wrong. We tilted the cot under which he was lying and saw what had happened. There he lay, all huddled up with his hands pressed against his heart. His hands and an overcoat that was spread under him were bloodstained. One hand firmly grasped a sharp cot spring, which he had used to pierce his own heart.

Now we knew why a few days ago he had begged us to help him detach a spring from the cot. He had not enough energy left in him to do it himself. Then he had sharpened one end of the spring against the cement floor, explaining that he was making an awl with which to repair his hopelessly worn-out footwear.

We called the guards. We all rose to attention, tearfully and with profound deference, as we sent him on his final journey to an unknown grave.

On the following day we refused to touch any food. Two days later the cots were removed from all the cells. This obviously was done in order to prevent any similar occurrences; for even prior to the Savchuk incident several inmates in other cells had committed suicide by hanging themselves from the uppermost cot by means of a rope made of strands from old socks or strips from shirts or towels.

Interrogation

TIME PASSED ON, but for us each day meant nothing but wretchedness and hopeless despair. The last ray of hope for rescue was clouded out and we resigned ourselves to this hell-hole without any brighter prospect for the future.

And then came the day. Around midnight the door opened and a guard came in, with a notebook in his hand. There was a long pause, calculated to fray the nerves.

Then followed the laconic question: "Any letter P's?"

We began to call out the names. When I came forward the guard asked me my Christian name and surname, then I dressed hurriedly for the interrogation, feeling a nervous chill go through me.

"Faster!" prompted the guard; and in a few minutes I left the cell with the sympathetic gaze of my fellow-inmates following me.

In the corridor there were a few more strange people. We were all led to the exit. The fresh air outside felt like a healing balm after the horrible stench of the cell. The sky was filled with myriads of twinkling stars, reminding me of better days gone by; and then came a feeling of bitter grief and ominous foreboding.

In the locked and brilliantly lighted court of the prison building into which we were hustled there stood one of those Black Crows which were so often evident on the streets of Kiev. The commander of the guards went through our names again and we were packed into the compartments of the "Crow." The back doors of this Black Crow were closed, the motor was started, and the machine drove off into the darkness.

Sitting down was no pleasant experience; for the enclosure was so narrow that we had to pull in our shoulders. The vehicle shook so roughly that it was all we could do to prevent banging our heads against the walls. I tried to follow the route of the Black Crow and thus I noticed Lukianiv, Lviw and Great Zytomir Streets. When it reached Kreschatyk Street, the "Crow" slowed up, and then with a roar went up Institute and across the Lypky section. Here I lost the trail. Finally the doors of the Black Crow opened and we found ourselves in the inner court of the Kiev Regional NKVD on Rosa Luxembourg Street. Near the exit of the car stood two guards with pointed pistols. Two other guards led us into the basement of a one-storey brick building. There we were shoved into "dog-houses." We were forced to stand up since there was nothing to sit on. The guard warned us to keep silence. It was ominously quiet in the corridor.

About half an hour later the door of my "dog-house" opened, and a guard, but not the one who had brought me there, quietly asked me my Christian name and surname. While I was telling him he opened the door wider and told me to come out. A guard with a holstered pistol stood by. I was ordered to leave with my hands behind my back. Meanwhile the guard flourished his revolver menacingly. A glass-enclosed entrance door was opened by a guard and I was directed to an asphalt walk which led through a small park in the inner court.

The whole park was brilliantly lighted. Looking around timidly I noticed among the sparsely planted trees some guards with ever-ready rifles. Farther on was a high wall with barbed-wire enclosures. Just as in the prison, escape here was out of the question; especially with blood-hounds alert for action. In any case I did not think of escape at the time.

This forty or fifty yard walk led to the back entrance of the regional NKVD administration building. When I came to the door the guard replaced his revolver in the holster and opened it. He led me up to the corridor on the second floor. Even while I was ascending the stairs I heard a heart-rending chorus, such as cannot be put into words. From behind dozens of doors facing the long corridor there came blood-curdling cries and groans, mingled with sadistic curses.

"Will you write, you counter-revolutionist? Christ almighty, God damn you . . .!"

As I went along the corridor I could hear the same

kind of hideous expressions coming out of each room. A medley of sobs, cries, pleas and profane abuse, giving one a horrible feeling of helplessness and depression.

Finally we halted, and our guard, opening a door, ordered me to enter.

I stepped into a circle of brilliant light which fell on me from the reflector of a lamp on a writing-table near the opposite wall. I was blinded momentarily by its strong glare and so could not see the prosecutor behind the table. I remained beside the door; but the guard moved forward to get the prosecutor's signature on the order. Then he left the room.

Now I was face to face with the prosecutor. He asked me my name and ordered me to sit down at a small table two or three yards away from where he sat. After a while he became dimly visible to me but from where he was he could see me only too plainly, even to the slightest twitch of my face.

He had a bulky file in front of him. Behind him was a window shaded by a dark blind. And inside the window was a strong wire netting.

Ignoring me completely, the investigator began to fumble among the papers in the file. This old psychological game kept up for about fifteen or twenty minutes. Then he looked up at me and stared intently, lowering his glance after a while to the papers and shaking his head from side to side as if to say: "My, my, what a criminal!"

This silent cat-and-mouse play did what it was intended to do; it jangled my nerves and inspired fear. I looked at the file in front of the investigator and wondered how I could be guilty of so much crime. It seemed as if my life were a written book into which every day a list of felonies had been entered. I was still too naïve at the time to recognize the psychological trick of instilling panic by a display of bulky, bogus files.

Finally the investigator rose and took a few steps towards me.

"Do you know, Prychodko, that during the ten years you have lived in Kiev we have been checking on you? In this book all your counter-revolutionary activities are recorded. Now you have only two alternatives: death by shooting or else twenty-five years in a labour camp. If you sign a confession we won't shoot you; all you will get is the twenty-five years." He hinted that there might be an amnesty and that I might get a chance to see my son.

After delivering himself of this generous proposition he returned to his table, opened a drawer and pulled out a stack of papers. He set this stack on my little table, and handed me a pen.

"Now you just sit there and write out a trustworthy confession of your counter-revolutionary activity. Don't hide anything: this would not be healthy for you; in any case we know everything; we merely want your corroboration, and your repentance. Do you understand?"

I told him that I understood everything, and that I

could not write out a confession as I was not guilty.

"What did you say?" the interrogator roared. I repeated more loudly that there was nothing to write, unless it was that my seventy-three-year-old father had been arrested a month ago. The interrogator then ran back to his table, picked up a half-filled water pitcher and came at me with it like an enraged bull. I began to back away from him and as I reached the wall he hurled the pitcher at me with all the force at his command. I instinctively side-stepped and the pitcher was shattered to bits against the wall, splattering it as well as myself with water. With demoniacal rage the investigator rushed at me.

"Pick up the bits, you son of a bitch!" he yelled.

When I bent down to gather them up, he kicked me viciously in the back. The force of this surprise attack knocked me off balance and I flopped on the floor, cutting my left hand on a jagged piece of glass. Without rising I squeezed the deep cut with my right hand and the blood ran out of the wound quite freely. The investigator kept right on booting me ferociously and indiscriminately. Following the advice I received while in the cell, I began to yell at the top of my voice, but this did not stop my persecutor. It was not until my voice petered out and I began to wheeze, and blood was spattered over the floor and on my clothing, that the investigator stopped mauling me. He kept yelling at me to get up. I tried to rise but each effort caused great pain. I finally managed to lift my body up into a sitting position. He rushed at me again, kicking me viciously in the face.

"Get up, you counter-revolutionary!" he shrieked.

The force of the blow knocked me down again, but in order to avoid any more punishment I got up on my feet, staggered along and leaned against the wall. I felt nauseated at the sight of the blood on my hands and clothing. The sleeve of my coat was saturated with it.

The investigator, noticing the blood still dripping from between my clenched fingers, went over to the table and pressed a button. Soon a guard rushed in.

"Send in an aide to bandage him up."

"I'll call him," answered the guard as he left the room.

The investigator slumped down behind the table and yelled, "I'll continue with you again; and when I do you'll write everything that is necessary!"

After this meaningful remark he shut up like a clam, drumming nervously with his fingers on the table.

In a few minutes the aide arrived, looking as sadistic as my assailant-investigator.

"What's wrong, comrade investigator?"

"Bandage him up!"

The aide seated me on a bench, rudely seized my wounded hand, slopped some iodine over the wound and then bandaged it. Having finished the job and having maintained a poker-face through it all, he left me alone with the investigator who got up again and came over to me, kicking a few pieces of glass under the table on the way. From the look on his face I realized that his physical attack on me was about to be renewed.

I sat on the bench like an animal about to be devoured.

"Now are you going to write?" he asked.

With a hoarse voice I told him that I had nothing to write since I was not guilty of any crime.

"Get up, damn you!" he blurted, raining heavy blows on my face with his clenched fists.

When I fell again to the floor he hurried to his table, opened a drawer, drew out a four-cornered chair-leg and began beating me on the head and body with it, all the while uttering the most vile Russian curses, which mingled with my own spasmodic cries. Some of my teeth were knocked out and I began to choke with blood. Finally I was knocked unconscious by a blow on the head, and so I do not know how long this attack lasted.

When I opened my eyes I found myself, somewhat dazed, sitting on the bench again, with the aide supporting me around the shoulder and holding a small bottle under my nose. The investigator was seated behind his table.

I found it hard to see anything. All the sight I had was through an unclosed slit in one eye. The other eye was swollen completely shut. When I tried to lift my eyelids I felt a burning pain. Perspiration flowed down my neck and I was seized with a sudden uncontrollable tremor. My whole body shook, and my teeth rattled as in a fever. I must have fainted. The aide forced some kind of tablet into my mouth which revived me and I regained consciousness.

The aide left the room without a word, but the investigator merely sat at the table with his head resting on his hands, as if sleeping. Notwithstanding the pains throughout my body, I was afraid to move or make a sound for fear of awakening him.

Forgetting for the moment my intense suffering, I inwardly prayed that God would cause him to fall into a deep slumber so that I would have at least a momentary respite. I studied the room furtively, and was glad to see through a small opening in the window shade that the day was dawning. I hoped against hope that this was the end of the investigation and that they would soon take me back to the prison.

In a few minutes the investigator raised his head. He looked at me indifferently, stretched himself luxuriously, and then silently left the room.

I remained alone. The pain became more acute. I felt extremely thirsty. My tongue seemed to stick to my palate. I yearned for even a few drops of water though I knew that was an impossible hope.

Someone came into the room; it was a maid. She placed a pitcher full of crystal clear water on the table without even bothering to glance my way. She gathered up the glass splinters from the floor, wiped up the water, and then silently left the room.

My attention was now glued to the pitcher of water. I had an uncontrollable urge to go over to the table and take a drink; but some strange power held me back. I felt that someone was watching me.

Thus I sat for about half an hour until a short young man entered, wearing NKVD uniform. He halted in front of me, shoved his hands into his pockets, swayed slightly on his feet and focussed me with an hypnotic stare, saying nothing the while. Then suddenly he ordered me to get up, directing toward me the usual Russian curses. I rose, holding on to the wall for support. He approached me rigidly with half-closed eyes.

"Now are you ready to write?" he asked.

When I told him there was nothing to write about, he began to hop around me like one insane, and to shove his fists in my face. Then he told me to open my mouth and stand erect against the wall. In order to avoid another beating I obeyed him. He then withdrew and sat down behind the table; but he soon got up again.

He came over to me, shouting:

"So that's the way you keep your mouth open? Open it wider!"

I did as I was told. He bent down at the knees and then rose straight up and spat right into my mouth.

This was the end of my endurance. My first impulse was to throw myself at him and sink my nails into his face; but caution warned that this would mean certain death; so I had to appease my rage with a few angry expectorations on the floor, for which he belaboured me soundly with a chair-leg.

This procedure was followed throughout the entire episode. Not for a moment was I allowed to sit down. When I leaned against the wall he ordered me to stand up straight and then applied the oak leg viciously to my back. My legs began to burn and I couldn't help leaning against the bench. When I asked him for a drink, all I got was a stream of filthy curses.

During half of the day he left the room twice for fairly lengthy periods and I was able to relax a little. I was greatly tempted to take a drink, and to sit down, but his warning withheld me. I would be allowed to sit down only when I wrote my confession.

His breakfast and dinner were brought into the room. He ate very slowly and with great relish, licking and smacking his lips meaningfully. This time the old game did not work as I had little appetite for anything. But when he lit a cigarette and asked me whether I wanted to have a smoke, that was another matter. I really did, and a drink as well; but I said I did not want any.

In the afternoon this apprentice's place was taken by another, who in no way differed from the former. Instead of spitting into my mouth, he thrust a wastepaper basket over my head and then yelled mockingly:

"Now you'll have to stand there like an idiot without moving until you are ready to write."

This continued until evening. Twice I got permission to enter the toilet, but always accompanied by a guard. I thought that perhaps I might be able to snatch a sip of water there; but the guard stayed too close.

In the evening, while I was still standing against the wall with the basket over my head, the investigator entered the room accompanied by another degenerate in

NKVD uniform. My ridiculous predicament caused them both to roar with laughter, with the investigator interjecting a bit of praise for his apprentice's cleverness. The latter, pleased with himself, began to chuckle. All of them began to make such remarks as: "Look at this caricature!"

When their line of banter wore out, the investigator asked his apprentice, "Well, what did he write?"

Receiving a negative reply, he turned to his new arrival.

"Can you imagine such a counter-revolutionary? All his life in and around Kiev he has been active in underground activity, and now he pretends to be innocent. But I'll deal with him yet in a manner he won't forget."

The investigator's colleague, feigning an expression of surprise and rage, ordered me to come forward; but when I hesitated a little he peppered me with insults. I took a few steps towards him and he came rushing at me so swiftly that he trampled on my toes. I began to back up, but he kept pushing ahead with his arms behind his back, making me retreat back to the wall.

Then he broke out with typical Russian police fury, "Now, will you write?"

And when I gave him the same monotonous negative answer, he struck me viciously in the face with the palm of his hand. This unexpected attack caught me unawares, and my head was thrust backward against the wall with such force that I slid down it to the floor in a semiconscious state. He pulled me away from the wall and began to stamp on my legs and body with his boots.

These blows seemed to be delivered at an accelerated rate. I instinctively clasped my head with both hands to protect myself and began to yell, or rather I should say, roar like a wild beast. The noise recalled to my mind the sounds I had heard from prisoners when I was passing down the corridor of this state torture chamber.

I was kicked unconscious again. I do not know how long this lasted, but when I recovered consciousness the investigator was standing over me, pouring water on my head from a pitcher. His assistant was sitting on a sofa regarding me casually.

As soon as I opened my eyes the investigator sarcastically remarked, "He still lives, curse him!" Then, to me, "Now, are you ready to confess?"

Since I did not answer he kicked me again, repeating the question. When I told him that I was guiltless, the beating was renewed.

I fainted again. When I revived I found myself slumped forward on a high square stool near the wall, so that my legs did not reach the floor. At first I did not realize my position but soon it all came back to me. The same excruciating pain. My legs began to swell and tingle as with fire. When I wanted to stand up the investigator ordered me not to move. When I begged for a little water he deluged me with a fresh stream of curses.

The investigator sat behind the table, turning over some papers. Meanwhile he repeatedly asked me when I was going to confess. I again stated that I had nothing to confess, that I had never engaged in any subversive activity. The investigator simulated interest in what I was saying, and I naïvely hoped that he would now deal reasonably with me. I asked him to investigate my report at the institution where I worked. He listened, nodding his head as if in assent.

My hopes were soon dissipated. He got up from the table, half-filled a glass with water, and sauntered slowly over toward me, acting as though he was going to give me a drink. His left hand held the glass of water. His right hand was in his trousers pocket. Suddenly he took his hand from his pocket and swung viciously at my head. I dodged and fell off the stool onto the floor.

After kicking me several times, he shouted, "Don't give me any of your fairy tales, but tell me about your counter-revolutionary work!"

I was more angry at my recurrent naïvety than at the cruel blows I received. The investigator ordered me to get up on the stool again, and then he slowly sipped the water in his glass, and returned to his chair.

Soon a chief entered the room. One could tell his rank from the General's insignia he was wearing, and the fact that the investigator immediately rose to attention, commanding me to do likewise. He asked whether I had signed any evidence; and on getting a negative reply he urged me to make an outright confession of my crimes and thus earn a lighter sentence. When I told him that I had nothing to confess, he pretended that he did not hear me and continued with his own line of questioning.

He incidentally remarked about my "tired look," but made no reference to the bloody welts on my face, or to my badly swollen eye. Then he politely suggested that I sit down on a nearby chair.

I took this seat and he walked back and forth in front of me, expounding the virtues of NKVD justice. He said he knew everything that was going on, but that he would like to see the prisoner confess of his own accord.

There was a pause in his grandiloquent eulogy of Soviet justice and his earnest exhortation of me. Then he reproved me for being so impolite as to sit on the whole chair in front of a superior and ordered me to sit on the edge of it. I complied and determinedly tried to get in a word by again denying my guilt. In answer to this the chief suddenly kicked the chair from under me, and I fell like a grain stalk to the floor. The chief, frantic with rage, booted me viciously.

When his wrath finally cooled off, he made this parting remark, "I'll use a different method with you next time. And you, comrade investigator, don't let him off too easy!"

My acquaintance with this NKVD chief taught me that there was little to choose between the justice of a high official and one lower down. The investigator seemed to take the chief's words to heart, for he kept me on the conveyor system, leaving me with his "apprentices" for four whole days, without water and food, alternately tortured with the chair leg, the boot and the fist. Dissatisfied with the methods employed the first night a more refined torture was initiated. My shirt was torn off and I was beaten with an oak paling from which twenty or thirty nail points protruded. The pain of these multiple pricks as each blow fell on my back was agonizing.

This is a picture of the NKVD investigation methods used in the "most democratic country of the world" in the spring of 1938, not in some remote cellar on the out-skirts, but in the "work room" of the official investigator of the Kiev Regional NKVD, right in the heart of the city on Rosa Luxembourg Street. It is just a glimpse into one of the countless torture-chambers with which the whole country was then honey-combed, as it is now.

Apart from the incessant beatings, the orders to confess, the tricks played on me, and the vile Russian curses, I never heard any concrete charges laid against me by the investigator. All he was interested in was a signed con-fession, irrespective of the truth, so that he could present his chief with evidence of his "high qualifications." He was not primarily interested in whether I had carried on counter-revolutionary activity, but sought rather to "ini-tiate" me and to transform me into a broken and docile serf for a Siberian slave camp.

In the days of Yezhov, this "prep-school" functioned in a myriad ways and places. A stupendous purge of all imaginary and potential enemies was being carried on, to-gether with a concurrent preparation of cheap labour power for the limitless lumbering and mining developments in Siberia. Stalin was preparing for the coming war. When one contemplates the prevailing slogan of the day, that the human being was the Soviet's greatest capital, the hypocrisy of the statement is nauseating. As an analogy one may recall the cynical and ridiculous slogan about the high standard of living during the years 1932–1933, when millions of peasants in the Ukraine, the richest country of the USSR, were dying from a state-organized famine.

Later on, when I thought over my first interrogation experience, I found it hard to believe that such a thing was possible; or that a giant, let alone an ordinary human being, could endure so much suffering.

I know that at the end of this torture I was unable to either stand or sit down. I just lay on the floor, all huddled up, groaning, while the investigator was pummelling me all over, trying to torture me into a confession.

Just before the conclusion of the interrogation he telephoned his wife to ask whether his son Igor was asleep. He told her to see to it that he was well covered, otherwise he might catch cold.

Perhaps this solicitous conversation was also calculated for psychological effect. However that might be, he came over and kicked me in the ribs.

"You will be sent to prison forthwith. There you will rot like a dog; meanwhile your wife will revel in other men's embraces."

He chuckled gleefully. This remark hurt me more than his punishment. If I had had the strength I would have bitten him in the leg; but in my helpless state I could only say that this ravishing was limited only to the wives of husbands who "worked" all night. This repartee evidently hit the spot, for he grabbed the ever-ready chair-leg and gave me another beating.

Then I fainted. When I revived, a couple of guards were dragging me by the arms out of the room. Somewhat hazily I heard the distant voice of the interrogator screeching, "Tomorrow I'll turn you into a bag of bones."

In the corridor they told me to get up, but since I was too weak, they hauled me by the arms along the corridor and down the stairs. Each bump was a source of added pain, but I no longer had the strength even to utter a groan.

Outside they held me up under the arms and again I found myself before the same wretched "dog-house" where they had held me before the interrogation. They threw me into it and closed the door.

Silence prevailed generally in the "dog-houses." The only evidence that they were occupied came from the intermittent sighs of the inmates.

In a few minutes the door opened and a guard peeped in. It was the same guard who had been on duty when I was brought out for questioning. He asked me whether I was the same man who had been in the "dog-house" during the last few days. Evidently he recognized me. When I answered him in the affirmative, he asked me whether I had had anything to eat during that time. I said

I had not, and asked him to give me at least a sip of water. He left quietly, closing the door behind him; but he returned shortly with a dipper of water and a piece of white bread.

"Here, take this, but keep quiet about it," he whispered in the Ukrainian language.

This gesture of compassion, evidently sincere and without ulterior motive, and the sound of my native tongue, so affected me that I began to weep like a child, although I had not shed a single tear during the inhuman persecution. He shook his finger cautiously in indication of silence; and then, picking up the dipper and shutting the door, he departed.

In about two hours they dragged me out to the Black Crow along with a few others, shoved us into separate compartments, and drove us through the streets of the silent city.

For the first time in my life I became completely lost in apathy, a sort of strange and absolute indifference to everything, even to life itself. Hitherto I could not readily imagine a person becoming a victim of indifference to life. If somebody had told me at that moment that our car was falling down some deep gorge and all I had to do to save myself was merely to lift a finger, I would not have done it. This profound depression lasted until our auto stopped before the gates of the prison. I was shocked out of this state by the sudden halt of the machine.

I was greeted in the cell with the same feeling displayed among long-separated relatives on being reunited. Some of the inmates got up and tried to comfort me as best they could; a cigarette from one, a piece of bread from another, and whispered questions about my interrogation from most of the others. Under a table in one of the corners they prepared a hidden resting-place for me.

My friend P. came over with a dipper of water and began to wash the blood off my face with a wet cloth; then he applied a compress to my swollen eye, out of which I could see nothing. He cursed and continued cursing the investigator for his brutality.

Placing his hand on my shoulder in brotherly fashion, he asked cautiously, "Did you write?"

An electric current of resurgent energy then seemed to go through me, and I felt proud of my ability to endure the torture without breaking.

"No!"

"That's fine. I'm glad to hear that you didn't give in to those snakes," he answered. He then helped me to get into my resting-place.

In spite of my great fatigue, I was unable to fall asleep for an hour, since my wounds still pained me. Besides this I was worrying about the forthcoming interrogation.

I finally did doze off into a fitful sleep. They did not wake me for the morning inspection, informing the guard that I was too ill; and so I rested until evening. When I awoke a light was burning in the cell. They gave me some bread, *balanda* and warm tea, and then I realized how hungry I was. Having finished the meal I began to relate the details of the interrogation. There was really nothing new in what I said, but they listened eagerly.

Late that night when the guard called others out for questioning, my heart began to thump with apprehension. The veins on my temples bulged, for was not this the day I was to be interrogated again? But I was not called either then or the next day. A whole month elapsed before it happened.

CHAPTER 9

The Case Against Me

ONE NIGHT they came for me — the same room, the same persecutor, the Russian, Nikitin. . . .

There was the same preliminary proposition put to me to confess to "counter-revolutionary activity," reinforced, of course, by liberal use of the chair-leg, but for some reason or other not quite so strongly applied as hitherto. I thought that perhaps the investigator had worn himself out, but I learned later that the punishment was toned down because of the fact that he now had two testifying witnesses against me, so that he could wind the case up against me, even if I did not sign a confession.

As a last resort, however, I was given still another beating to wrench a statement out of me; but when this was not successful he sat down behind his table and began to write out a finding, still charging me with nothing concrete.

After a few formal questions about my past, and that of my father and mother as well, he asked me whether I considered myself guilty by virtue of belonging to a

Ukrainian anti-Soviet organization. When I answered in the negative he entered it in the record. Then he asked me whether I knew D., and what were the nature of my anti-Soviet conversations with him. I told him how things were and how I knew D., but that I never had any such conversations with him. With the completion of this report my case was sent to the OSO, at Moscow. I was taken back to the prison, where I spent eight months before I was questioned again. It was only then that I was informed by a new investigator why I had been arrested.

Here are the facts. Before the Christmas holidays I wrote a letter to my friend D., a village school teacher, in which I invited him to come to Kiev and relax a bit. There wasn't the slightest mention of politics in the letter, nor had we ever talked politics, since he had never shown any interest in them.

During the execution of the wholesale plan of arrests at Romny, D. was caught in the net on the day that he received my letter. With a letter from Kiev in his pocket the investigator figured he had a good pretext. He soon began to capitalize on it, and it was not long before he had Mr. D., with all his good nature, confessing to the charge that I had influenced him to take part in a subversive organization.

This case was submitted to Kiev where it kept gathering momentum. Since I refused to testify falsely against myself the investigator in the district was ordered to find another witness. And thus it was that Mr. D.'s friend came into the picture. He was that other witness, but I had never seen him in my life before. At one of the sittings, and in my presence, he swore with downcast eyes that I had been instrumental in getting him to join the organization. This specious confession was even more doctored than the other. Perhaps the investigator was looking for a decoration for the "execution of special services to the party and the government." Incidentally, the confession added that one of my relatives who worked at the Academy of Sciences was also a member of this organization.

In his haste to get this matter off his hands, or else through mere inadvertence, the investigator did not have my relative arrested, but passed the case on to Moscow. The case was referred back for further investigation. Perhaps it was this prolongation of my incarceration in prison until the final settlement of the case that saved me from death.

After this final interrogation, I waited from day to day for the sentence. Sentences were usually given a week or two after the depositions were signed; or else the prisoners were shipped with their belongings to parts unknown without a pronouncement of sentence. That is what usually happened when a case came before an NKVD trio. The trio was composed of two NKVD officials and an investigator who presented the case and acted as prosecutor as well. Such trios functioned incessantly, especially under Yezhov. They passed sentences of death by the thousands.

Other thousands, mostly high-ranking military and administrative officials, had to go through a so-called court martial, a closed tribunal composed of top-ranking officials of the central NKVD administration. At such a court they merely called the prisoner and asked him one single question.

"Are you guilty?"

No excuses were tolerated; and as a matter of fact no one ever did try to exonerate himself, since every prisoner, prior to going before the military court, found himself in a room with his investigator, who threatened to tear his hide off if he tried to reverse his former admissions. This information was confided to us by a high official of the North-West Railroad Administration, the communist Bolotin, who went through a military tribunal experience and returned from it to our cell with white hair and a twenty-five-year sentence. Ninety per cent of these prisoners got death sentences. The other ten per cent, the more fortunate ones, got from fifteen to twenty-five years imprisonment.

There was also another court, the so-called "special board." Only about five per cent of the prisoners ever come before it; namely, such as were unable to deny their written confessions. The "special board" was reputed to be a civil court, but in reality NKVD officials in civilian clothes presided there. Among the members of this board was a "representative of the workers," who was just an NKVD stooge masquerading as a judge.

The "special boards" did not sit very long, and nearly always behind closed doors. Once in a while, however, the court was open to the public for propaganda purposes to show them the "enemies of the people." In such cases the prisoners were kept in separate cells with more space and better ventilation, and they were fed better to give them a more human appearance. If any signs or marks of persecution were still visible, they were treated medically. Then they were brought before the court and asked, "Have you heard of anybody being beaten in prison during interrogation?"

The usual forced answer was "No, there were a lot of people with me, but none of them was ever mishandled physically."

These methods were deemed necessary to squelch any rumours in the outside world. The "special board" sometimes freed a few prisoners, although under threat of death if they disclosed the secrets of the NKVD prisons. With such a Damoclean sword hanging over them they lived in continual fear; and they were often forced to become stooges of the NKVD.

Awaiting Sentence

MONTHS PASSED, and Yezhov kept on destroying countless victims. Countless sealed trains wended their way without a trace to the far north, carrying millions of serfs for the slave camps. In the cellars and silent ravines tens of thousands fell victim to shots in the nape of the neck from the NKVD bandits. And within the prison walls the old preliminary work went on incessantly. New prisoners kept pouring in to replace those sent away.

At the beginning of summer there were one hundred and thirty-two prisoners in our small cell. There was hardly standing room, let alone a place to sit or sleep. It was stuffy beyond endurance, with the sun beating down on the roof and the window shutters closed. We stripped our clothes off, but even that didn't help much. We sweated profusely, using rags to wipe ourselves, and then wringing them out into bowls at our feet. These bowls were handed from one person to another and emptied into the urinal. Our bodies were covered with red itchy spots which bothered us all day long. Even when fresh air did blow in at night, myriads of bed-bugs came out of invisible crevices and prevented sleep.

To slake the thirst of one hundred and thirty-two persons, all we got was a six-gallon iron bucket of water in the evening. It is hard to picture the state of mind with which we awaited this small dole of water. We poured it carefully into cups as if it were some priceless nectar. The water, of course, was locked all day long in the wash rooms. We had to go there in our bare feet across a lot of stinking filth to bring it with us to the cell, thus befouling the air still more.

When we were out for our exercise I glanced at my fellow-prisoners. They looked like illusory, skinny, wax skeletons. I was afraid to ask anybody what I looked like.

Some of the inmates did not have the strength to endure this sort of life, so they were taken away, we knew not where, and their places filled with others. Any protest against this order of things was punished with a sound beating, for the superintendents had full power of control to use us as they saw fit.

One day two peasants were brought into our cell directly following an investigation at Brovari near Kiev. They told us about a terrible "death combine" operating in the Darnitsky forest behind a barbed-wire enclosure. In damp cellars of about forty square yards in area, two hundred and fifty prisoners were incarcerated, with standing room only, in the stench of their own sweating bodies, and with hardly any water to drink or anything to eat.

Near these cells the torture chambers worked day and night, and the cries of the tortured victims kept on incessantly. Their feet were seared with hot irons, air was pumped into their stomachs with motor-cycle pumps, needles were forced under their finger-nails, and they were beaten over the most delicate parts of their body with an oak ruler. This in the Twentieth Century, in the "most happy country in the world"! Several corpses were carried out from the cells every day, and in the dead of night many more were taken away to the Darnitsky forest to eternal peace. . . .

Their places in the cells were soon filled with other prisoners.

In the outside courtyard of the torture chamber there was a deep well. One day when they were marching a group of prisoners by this well, two of them broke out of line and dived into it head first.

Following this incident, the well was covered over with boards.

When the Nazis invaded the Ukraine, they uncovered a mass burial place at Vynnytza, where thousands of corpses had been thrown. The same evidence was discovered in the Darnitsky forest near Brovari, although here they had no time to disinter the bodies, since they had already begun to retreat from the Ukraine; and they had to cover up all traces of their own atrocities.

And so at Brovari thousands of unknown persons lay dead without benefit of decent burial or a cross to mark their graves. Somewhere in the night many bereft mothers and orphaned children must have been waiting in vain and shedding bitter tears. . . .

One day, the door was opened during the daytime. The guard called out the names of three people and ordered them to come along with their belongings. I was one of the three. Since it was rare for a prisoner to leave with his belongings during the day, the hope that this might mean freedom began to surge up again. We began to dress excitedly, the other inmates passing messages from one to the other for us to deliver to their relatives. We promised to deliver them, but doubts began to creep in about our freedom. I felt as if I were electrified. Something was about to happen. When prisoners were going to be questioned they did not take their belongings with them, and why were we asked out in the daytime?

When we got out into the corridor, twelve men were already standing there in a row. We were told to fall in line; and so were the inmates who had been led out of the other cells. But we all still held fast to the naïve supposition that freedom was in the offing.

I asked the man next to me quietly what the charge against him was. It appeared that he and his neighbour on the other side were charged with espionage. This rather dampened my hope for liberation; but not altogether. There was still a thin ray of hope filtering into my consciousness.

When about thirty inmates were finally rounded up

from the various cells, we were led down stairs until we came to the exit door of the building. The guard rapped on the little window in the door to draw the attention of the guard outside.

We were doomed to sudden disillusionment. The door did not open. Instead, the guard was handed a key through the window. We were led down a stairway. The guard unlocked an iron-bound oak door, then a steel-grated one, and we found ourselves in a large basement cell with a very damp cement floor. This actually was the cellar of a former prison chapel. By evening about five hundred people were packed into this place. By rapping on the walls we learned that the neighbouring cells were also being filled up. By now there was no illusion about our fears, and we waited for the worst.

In the middle of the night, when we had settled ourselves to sleep, if possible, the door bar rasped and the superintendent of the prison, the prosecutor Ivanov, burst into the cell, accompanied by three others in NKVD uniforms.

With eyes glaring he shrieked: "Get up, you sons of bitches, you counter-revolutionaries! What kind of a noise is this? I'll show you, you . . . !"

We rose and stood silently before him, heads bent low. Some of the inmates found it hard to know whether this was a bad dream or reality, since there had been no noise in the cell. Ivanov hurled a few more curses and epithets at us, and then ordered the guards to put ten men into the airless *kartser*. He indicated ten of the inmates standing nearest to him. Uttering another filthy oath, he then left with his fellow officials. The guards took the designated ten men out with them.

We sat down again. Some one in the corner, unable to stand the strain, started to sob hysterically, but his neighbours soon had him under control.

The next morning eight of the men came back from the *kartser*. They were hardly able to drag their legs along. In the *kartser* they had been stuffed into stone compartments with hermetically sealed doors where the only parts of their bodies they could move were their heads. When they lost consciousness the doors were opened for a few seconds to allow air in. As soon as they revived, the doors were shut again. This process was repeated throughout the whole night. The two who failed to return most likely perished from suffocation, since we never heard of them again.

The next day we had nothing to eat; but in the evening they brought us two vats of soup and fifteen loaves of bread for the lot of us.

During the following fifteen days we were held to a very restricted routine. There were no outdoor exercises. We were shuffled around to the various prison cells, but never to the ones we had been in previously.

Later on, after the liquidation of Yezhov, Hulakov, a former chief of the 5th Division of the Kiev Regional NKVD, made his appearance in our cell. He told us that a mass shooting of prisoners was planned by the NKVD at that time.

CHAPTER 11

The Purge of the Purgers

WE FIRST LEARNED about Yezhov's disappearance when we noticed the box for complaints to Yezhov missing from the courtyard wall. The prison inmates viewed this news very optimistically, hoping that the wave of terror was receding.

And that is exactly what happened. The purge had run its course. There were now enough victims and so it was time for a pause. The main instigator of this purge had been the goblin-like Yezhov, formerly Stalin's personal secretary. As Stalin's direct appointee he must have received his instructions from his chief. If results were the criterion, Stalin must have been satisfied with his choice; for in a short time hundreds of thousands had been shot, and millions mobilized for the Siberian slave camps and the mines of Kolyma. When this horrible orgy ended, the Kremlin must have felt secure. In order to sanctify himself and establish his "infallibility" among the people, Stalin then started a "Purge of the Purgers" by announcing at one of the meetings of the party that the policy of the party had been "twisted" by certain officials of the NKVD who were "enemies of the people."

And thus it happened that the man who not so long ago was called the "beloved *Narkom* of Stalin" perished in one of the undisclosed cellars as a twister of Stalin's directions. But the great father lived on as the infallible chief.

In order to conceal the real facts from the people, one tenth of one per cent of the prisoners incarcerated prior to the liquidation of Yezhov were liberated, and even a few hundred returned from Siberia. This was all done for propaganda purposes, as if to say: "The innocent ones are freed, but the real enemies are left in prison. You have been rescued from them by the most wise Stalin."

As a further propaganda measure, a few NKVD officials were thrust into prison on the pretext that they were "twisters of the party's policy," but thousands of others were awarded decorations of honour.

I met two of these masterful "twisters" in the prison. One of them was a chief of the Chrystynivska NKVD area during Yezhov's reign, but I do not remember his name. The other was Hulakov, a chief of the 5th Division of the Kiev Regional NKVD. Fearing revenge, they tried desperately to ingratiate themselves with the more influential inmates in the cell, and they frequently divulged many secrets of the service.

The Chrystynivska chief related that at the beginning of the Yezhov period he had been ordered to arrest 3,800 people in the area. He had arrested all those who at one time or another had been imprisoned for political crimes and then freed; and also those who were under suspicion on information supplied by the *seksots*. But he still did not have the required number and it was necessary to exceed the quota in order to make a good showing. He then proposed to the heads of the village councils that they supply him with lists of those who should be arrested. The quota was over-subscribed; and then the usual "confession" was extracted with the aid of an oak chairleg. The Chrystynivska chief expected to be rewarded for his "service," but he wound up by being included in the quota desired by the regional chief!

Hulakov was a bigger fish. Formerly he had been a responsible member of a spy ring in Iran, where he masqueraded as a small official of the Soviet Embassy. Later on he was one of the eleven who kidnapped General Koutepov in Paris. For this "service" he had received the military order of the "Red Flag." The award was recorded in the usual phraseology: "For performance of especially important tasks for the party and the government." Now the investigators rewarded him with a few bloody decorations on his back and made him sign a confession about his sabotage within the NKVD organization, and so he disclosed to us many secrets of the operation of the NKVD.

For instance, he told us about a garage in the court of the regional NKVD on Rosa Luxembourg Street in Kiev, into which Black Crows, loaded with prisoners, were driven at night. The back door of the Black Crow opened on to a stairway leading down into a cellar, where, from a dark corner, there came the notorious shot in the neck. This shot cannot be heard by any passing pedestrian, for the sound is drowned out by the Crow's motor running at full blast. In this and in other ways, in Kiev alone, from November 1937 to February 1938, over ten thousand "enemies of the people" were liquidated.

Hulakov explained that the reason for his being in prison was that he did not listen to orders and took too humane an attitude towards the prisoners under his investigation. We were a little doubtful about that, for outwardly Hulakov looked like a typical NKVD-man. But we gave him the benefit of the doubt, since there were some rare exceptions even among that cruel and callous group. Later on, when some inmates of the other cells heard about his presence in the prison, they told us that Hulakov was one of the worst of the persecutors. Then he was boycotted in the cell. We did not molest him, however, for fear of reprisal by the prison authorities, who would not tolerate this attitude towards a former colleague. Finally he was badly beaten by the prisoners as he was being transported to the Dispersal Depot.

After the disappearance of Yezhov there was no change in the prison regime, unless it was that the beating at the investigations subsided a little, but even this small blessing did not apply to everyone. Generally speaking the state torture chamber functioned as usual. The prisoners still remained in the same unenviable position, waiting from day to day for a change in the situation, and trying to find evidences of it in a variety of insignificant events.

I remember one of our comrades returning from one of those gruelling third degrees. He was a pitiful sight. It was early morning, and many sleepy heads rose to ask how he fared.

Assuming an attitude of profound secrecy, he answered, "A change of situation!"

When more heads lifted up excitedly, he continued solemnly, "Hitherto they used a chair-leg on me, but not any more. Today I was beaten with a table-leg."

Some of us smiled at this, but others merely fell back gloomily into their places again.

The days rolled on monotonously. Our hopes for a change began to fade. Perhaps there was a change for those enjoying freedom outside; but not for us.

signed. The court ignored him completely and the prosecutor was told to go on. He contended that on the basis
of the "most democratic law" Borziak was the "fiercest
enemy of the people"; that he was the true son of his
father, who had owned one hundred and twenty-five
acres of land. As a landowner he was branded as one
who had woven a "bloody web of intrigue around the
whole of the USSR and, in conjunction with bloody
world-capitalism, aimed at the downfall of the Soviet
regime." And the judge, who was supposed to administer
the law impartially, but who in reality warped facts to
suit the ideas of the Soviet authorities, gave Borziak
a death sentence. Dmytro Borziak lived for fifty-nine
days in terrible suspense and agony in the Lukianiwska
prison in Corridor Number 6, reserved for those sentenced to death.

From eleven o'clock every night till four o'clock in
the morning, he and hundreds of others went through
the hell of waiting for death. In every cell deathlike
silence prevailed. With bated breath the inmates listened
intently for the approaching footsteps and the turning
of the key. And then the guards came, looking each
prisoner over in turn. Then came a pause — a deliberately
prolonged pause before the final call to death. . . .

Some of the weaker ones, unable to stand it, cried out
hysterically. Such cases were usually pacified out in the
corridor by the refined methods of the guards.

Sometimes one could hear the piteous voices of these
unfortunate people calling out: "Farewell, brothers!"

And then the voices would suddenly die down, as if the prisoners were being beaten into silence.

There was no peace in the cell until after four A.M. Then the inmates would lie down on the cement floor and drop into a horror of bad dreams.

For Borziak it was like this for fifty-nine days, but for some there was as much as a three-month death wait. In rare cases the death sentence was reduced to ten or more years of slave-labour.

Here was a person, rescued from this hell by some "miracle," undergoing a new resurrection. I recall the zest for life displayed by Borziak when he used to relate certain incidents in his life before he was arrested. I also remember the deep affection with which he spoke about his relatives, and his son. He frequently talked about his friend, Theodosy Osmachka.

"Just imagine, Nicholas, what kind of a man he was," said Borziak. "For months he holes up in a crypt creating the most beautiful things. Just listen."

And then Borziak would quietly recite whole passages from Osmachka's translations of Shakespeare, as well as his colourful verses. "And all this was composed while in hiding! Just imagine what masterpieces he could have turned out if he had been given a free hand in a free Ukraine!"

During all these conversations Borziak's eyes would blaze with subdued fire. His speech was frequently interrupted by violent fits of dry coughing. His handkerchief was sometimes smeared with spots of blood. This,

however, did not bother him inwardly. He kept cling-
ing to the hope that another miracle would enable him to
return home again.

Two weeks later Borziak was called out into the corridor to hear the following announcement: "Death sentence changed to fifteen years in a political isolator."
His hope and his new-found happiness faded away.

"Now I shall never see the Dnieper from Volodymyr
Hill, nor will I be able to gather my son into my arms,"
he said.

The next day Borziak was taken away. Two weeks
went by. Then the prison grapevine informed us that
Dmytro Borziak had committed suicide by cutting his
wrists with a piece of glass.

We, who had grown to love him, honoured his memory with deep silence and many fists were clenched in
righteous but futile indignation against the bestial regime.

CHAPTER 13

A Visit from My Sister

A FEW MORE MONTHS passed by monotonously. We lived through them almost statically. We felt like baggage, stored and forgotten in a cellar.

One night I was suddenly called out for questioning. There was a new investigator, but he differed little in his methods of interrogation from the others. Nevertheless, the punishment was less severe, and I wondered if this indicated some change in the situation.

At first the investigator demanded a signed confession of my counter-revolutionary activity. Then he began questioning me about my relative at the Academy of Sciences, and about those who had testified against me. Since he did not get any admissions from me, he began to write out his report, and then let me go back to the prison.

The next day he called me again, but he did not beat me or ask me any more questions. He merely told me to read the incriminating testimony. This was not the usual procedure in Yezhov's era.

I returned again to the prison. Four months later I was summoned by the superintendent of the corridor who read that on the basis of a resolution of a special decree of the OSO NKVD of the USSR, I was sentenced by Article 54.11 to ten years' imprisonment in the Corrective Labour Camps of the NKVD for activity in a Ukrainian nationalist-underground organization. I accepted this verdict with almost perfect indifference, since by this time I had become inured to my imminent doom. After spending these wretched months in jail, even hell was welcome, as long as I could get out of my cell.

Preparations soon commenced for our transfer to the convict shipping-depot. All sentenced persons were taken out of the cells in groups and led into larger rooms with a capacity of two or three hundred people, elbow-room not included. There we were given better food. We were told that before the train pulled out we would be allowed a ten-minute meeting with our relatives. Such "humanitarianism" was astounding. We thought the announcement was made more for mockery than anything else. But in a few days they began to call us out for these meetings in small groups. We anticipated it with joy and fear, since no one knew who was left in the outside world for us to talk to. Those who were not called out wondered whether they would see any of their relatives again.

I had spent over twenty months in jail under the grimmest kind of isolation from the outside world. It was only because fifty rubles were deposited in my account each month that I knew that any one of my close relatives was still alive.

It is hard to put into words the simultaneous feeling of joy and fear which possessed me when my turn came. As I went along the corridors my legs were as heavy as lead. My arms felt numb. My heart throbbed violently, and then it seemed as if it had stopped completely. I kept thinking of one thing only — whether I would see my wife and son.

The room to which I was led, along with two others, was partitioned off from the corridor by a thin wire netting. I focussed my eyes on that screen with great trepidation.

Nobody was in the room. A few feet from this screen there was a barrier, and a guard kept marching up and down between the two, watching us. He halted midway, rudely ordering us to maintain silence during our meeting, and not to disclose the conditions of our stay in prison, nor say anything about the interrogation. The penalty for disobeying this order was "discontinuance of the meeting and severe punishment."

We obeyed him, but we kept watching the door of the room opposite us. In a few minutes it opened and my sister entered the room with some strangers. My wife and son were not present. Bitterly disappointed, I leaned against the wire netting, grasping it with my hands to avoid falling down. Spasms of faintness seized me, and it was all I could do to keep from sobbing.

My sister approached the barrier, somewhat abstractedly scanning it, until she finally recognized me.

"Oh, my dear brother," she said in alarm. "What have they done to you?"

She started to cry.

Her tears drew me out of my state of numbness, and I asked, "Where are my son and wife? What happened to them?"

"They are still alive," she said. "Your wife was forced to renounce you as an enemy of the people; that is why they didn't come. But I came . . . Mother is alive, they are all alive . . . but they don't live in Kiev any more . . . don't you worry, my dear brother . . . oh, how unfortunate you are."

She broke down and started to cry again.

Forgetting my own plight, I began to soothe her.

"Don't cry, little sister; I've been a little ill . . . now I feel quite well . . . nothing is the matter with me . . . don't tell Mother that I do not look well, for that would only make her feel worse. The past is behind me. I shall go away, but I'll find work at my old profession and everything will be all right. Only don't cry, my little dove!"

I spoke a few more words of comfort, which quieted her a little. She was almost as unfortunate as myself in her eternal waiting by the prison gate.

When the guard had moved on a little way, she whispered, "Is it true that they beat you?"

"No, no," I said. "Not any more . . ."

I asked her to console Mother and the others. I longed so much to touch her with my hands and kiss her, and my heart ached to be with my dear ones. But the obstacles of the wire netting and the barrier were between us, and so was the guard . . .

Avoiding various questions by my fellow cell-mates, I trudged to my corner, sat down on my dirty bedding, and wept bitter tears. My heart throbbed with pain. I now felt the full bitterness of being separated from my kin, my kin in freedom, who were probably not much more fortunate than myself. For two days I ate nothing. I kept to myself and my own wretched thoughts.

CHAPTER 14

Journey to Siberia

ON AN EVENING in November, 1939, we were taken out in threes from the convict-depot building and then loaded onto trucks surrounded by guards with ever-ready rifles. Guards, guards everywhere, even on the running-boards of our trucks.

On a hillock not far from the prison gates stood a group of women and children. Someone must have passed the word that the convict group was about to leave. They eagerly scanned the prisoners in the trucks, excitedly waving us farewell and trying to pick out their own near relatives. This sight was like balm to our hearts, and we just as eagerly reciprocated in kind. My neighbour, who sat near the side of the truck, suddenly cried out, "Hannusia!" and waved his hand.

The head guard who stood at the front of the truck yelled, "Hit the snake on the hands!"

The guard who sat next to us struck him viciously on the shoulders with the butt of his rifle. The truck pulled out faster, so that we could only imagine the tears flowing down Hannusia's face.

On the supply-train tracks at the Lukianiwska Freight Station we were packed into freight cars with grated windows — forty-two persons to the car. The doors were quickly shut, so that no onlooker would be able to tell what kind of freight was being packed in the evening twilight into the long train. It was well guarded by faithful, picked men with trained Siberian police dogs.

As we were strictly forbidden to look out of the windows, we peeped through a crevice that we discovered in the door, looking intently for any silhouettes of our relatives in the distance, although so far away it would have been impossible to recognize anyone. We did, however, notice that the guards posted on the road which ran parallel to the tracks kept ordering the people away.

When complete darkness fell, we heard the wailing of a woman coming from that direction.

"Andrew, Andrew darling, I am here. I will always be with you . . . our son is well . . ."

This same voice and these same words repeated and repeated through the whole night, like a lonely sea gull calling plaintively over the misty expanse. Evidently the guards kept chasing her away, for often after a lengthy pause we would hear it all over again from a different direction. From farther down the train an answer broke out, but it was soon drowned out by the vigorous knocks of rifle butts against the walls of the box-car.

The voice seemed to die down and then revive again, and it intensified our own grief.

We lay down on the bare board floor, or on the wooden slats, but were not able to fall asleep. I do not know whether it was because of the change from the stuffiness of the cell, or because in the quiet of the night we kept listening for some familiar voice coming out of the dark.

The transport train remained stationary until morning, and then it pulled out. But before it really started for its unknown destination it was shunted onto one of the side-tracks of the Central Freight Station of Kiev, where it remained for almost twenty-four hours. Again at night we heard heart-rending voices calling to their relatives from the darkness.

We were thirsty beyond endurance, for they gave us four salted fish each and a bit of bread, but not a single drop of water. In the morning we began to clamour for water, at first timorously, and then more loudly. In a few minutes the whole two thousand prisoners in the train raised their voices in unison, as if by command.

"Wa-ter . . . wa-ter . . . wa-ter!"

This time the gun-stocks on the walls did not have any effect. Peering cautiously through the grated window, we noticed that railroad workers and casual pedestrians were gathering around the box-cars and on the railway ties farther away. Attracted by the commotion, they waved their hands at us in sympathy. The guards did not dare to let a demonstration like this get out of hand, and so they opened the doors and deposited a pail of water in every box-car. The prisoners then quieted down, and in two hours the wheels of the train began to rattle rhythmically over the rails: "To Siberia . . . to Siberia . . . to Siberia!"

The train was well guarded. Guards with machine-guns and police dogs were stationed in the back and front box-cars. Guards were also planted on the platforms between the cars. Our train didn't stop at the smaller stations. The guards kept jumping from one car to another in order to satisfy themselves that the "enemies of the people" did not break open any boards in the roof; while others were inspecting the walls by tapping on them with long-handled wooden hammers. This procedure was followed at every long stop. We were given a little water en route and some kind of hot *balanda*, but the usual menu was bread and salted fish.

We sought every possible opportunity to send messages back home. One of our greatest treasures was a piece of wrapping paper and a pencil which one of the prisoners had managed to hide away during the search. A few had several sheets of cigarette paper. Messages were written on one side and addresses on the other. These papers were tied to a crust of bread and thrown out through the grating in the window at a time when the train was stationary or had slowed down considerably, in the hope that some railway workers or pedestrians would pick them up and somehow send them on to their destination. Later on I learned when I was back home that all my eight messages, thus thrown out the window, starting with Kharkov and passing Sverdlovsk, were duly delivered. There was no doubt that the finders of these messages knew what kind of "enemies of the people" the "train of special destination" was carrying. It often happened, during the longer stops, that someone from a group of spectators would try to give us some food: but such attempts were usually foiled by the guards.

There is one episode of the journey that stands out in my memory. Once our train stopped at a large station in the Urals. The stop was not well timed; for right opposite us a Far East Pullman Express stopped simultaneously. Through the large windows of some first-class coaches we could see many well-dressed, fat and jovial passengers, no doubt members of the new Soviet "aristocracy." The tables were laid out with many varieties of tasty food, which we could not have conjured up even in our imaginations.

Noticing us, some of these passengers rose up and began eyeing us as if we were the inmates of some zoological garden, while others must have sympathized with us, knowing full well that the same fate might meet them at any time.

Right opposite our window stood a military figure of high rank, with three decorations on his chest. He contemplated us rather sadly, and when the express began to pull out, he cautiously waved his hand at us in a farewell greeting, which went unnoticed by his colleagues. He evidently realized that with all his services, the day might come any time when he would be riding on one of those "Stalin Specials."

And now we were pulling into the *taiga*, or Siberian forest. For hundreds of miles the landscape remained unchanged, forest upon forest without end. Long trains loaded with lumber and mineral ore passed us by. They spoke eloquently of what awaited us. Frequently we saw barracks or tents among the trees, surrounded by barbed-wire. At various points in these enclosures, guard-towers rose up; and in the distance we could see the figures of armed guards, dressed in long sheepskin overcoats and high felt boots.

At the stations in the forest we now saw different kinds of workmen. They were pitiful looking creatures, emaciated almost beyond recognition, dressed in tattered rags. Their feet were bound with cloth, over which they wore *lapti*, made from the inner bark of trees. They loaded lumber onto cars, laid branch railway lines, or did other kinds of heavy labour. Near every group of workmen stood a guard, who not only watched them, but goaded them on to work faster.

When they saw our train, these slave-labourers nodded their heads sympathetically, and, with an eye on their guards, asked us where we were from and what was new in the outside world. Somewhat reticently they asked us whether we had a spare piece of bread or anything to smoke. When we asked them about the conditions of their work they merely waved their hands resignedly. Indescribably dirty and grotesquely clad, they were a picture of utter indifference to life.

And as a complement to this scene was the endless, inhospitable and gloomy *taiga*, eternally covered with deep snow, in the midst of which, here and there, were the barbed-wire enclosures of the "Corrective NKVD Labour Camps," with their watch-towers. They would make an appropriate emblem on the banner of the Great Prison of Nations, the USSR.

After many days of travelling across the *taiga*, our train halted in the midst of a large, snow-covered clearing. Not far from us there was a group of barrack buildings, enclosed by barbed-wire.

The guards opened the doors and ordered us to come out. We jumped into the brilliant snow, sinking down into it to our waists, momentarily happy in being able to breathe some fresh air. We could hardly take in this very cold air, and yet somehow we filled our lungs with it again and again.

The transit muster camp of Sama, called after the name of the nearest large station, was built on a great clearing in the midst of the *taiga*, and was enclosed by a double fence of barbed-wire. There were high watch-towers all around this camp. Inside the enclosure there were long, log barracks with low ceilings; and inside the barracks there were rows of double-decker bunks. Between the bunks there was a narrow aisle, and in the centre of each barrack stood an iron stove.

On the day before, a previous contingent had departed, and so some of the barracks were empty. There was room in each barrack for three hundred new inhabitants. At first it appeared as if we had a little freedom, for we were allowed to walk about the camp grounds without escort. We had not hoped in vain for a change in situation, for here it was.

Besides us there were a few hundred others in the camp who had arrived only a few days previously and who were now awaiting a new destination. They warned us about certain criminals in the camp who had to be watched at night to prevent them from stealing our clothes. In our journey around this camp we came across about two hundred prisoners from southern Georgia, mostly descendants of the original Georgians. Their faces were pale and emaciated, but their eyes blazed with an indomitable spirit and a fierce desire for revenge on those who had dragged them out of their sunny, mountain *auls* and shipped them to this gloomy, cold and inhospitable country. Every day three or four corpses were taken out of their barrack, for they were unable to stand this fifty below zero weather, and many of them contracted tuberculosis. Apart from an occasional aspirin there was no medical aid in the camp. Life was held very cheap here, for in the *taiga* countless graves could be dug, and no one would be able to find them under the deep Siberian snows.

We spent the whole day breathing in the fresh air and enjoying a moment of illusory freedom. As I walked about the camp grounds it seemed as if a guard were following me. I glanced around several times to see whether this were so.

At night we set a watch by the door because of what we had heard about criminals. But even so we were not able to fall asleep, for myriads of bed-bugs began to attack us. There was no escape from them except in deep slumber, to which some of us succumbed after a while.

But our sleep was soon disturbed by a commotion in the neighbouring barracks. We rushed out to see if we could be of any help. The barrack which we entered was pitch dark. Near the door and in the middle of the barrack men were milling about with flailing arms, shouting. Their numbers were reinforced by prisoners coming in from other barracks to the aid of their friends. The fight continued for half an hour, ending with the defeat of the criminals, who hurriedly retreated to their own barracks, leaving one of their own number dead upon the floor. Three men on our side received knife wounds, from which two of them died the next morning.

The camp guards ignored the affair completely, since they knew this was not a rebellion. They merely picked up the three dead bodies and disposed of them without comment. The next night we were not molested for the simple reason that the criminals knew that they were out-numbered.

In the morning we were given two and a quarter pounds of bread and then ordered to form ranks outside the barracks. We waited an hour out in the cold until the guards approached the gates. They dumped a pile of old tattered garments nearby, and these were distributed to the prisoners who had little clothing and whose feet were bound with pieces of rags. Evidently these garments were stripped off the numerous dead bodies before they were buried, and they served not only to clothe living corpses, but also as the only mementoes left by the dead ones.

Outside the gates a large armed convoy awaited us with leashed blood-hounds. Actually we never saw any armed guards on the camp grounds; for the defence regulations were made in anticipation that the prisoners might some time in their despair attack the guards and disarm them.

Before our departure the leader of the convoy warned us that anyone falling out of line would be shot like a dog. We started out along a narrow road, hewn through the limitless *taiga*, walled on both sides by a thick growth of forest trees. This long column of three thousand persons extended as far as the eye could see; and beside it marched guards with their carbines and dogs, spaced at intervals of about fifty yards.

Although the road was already beaten by a preceding contingent we sank in places so deep into the snow that we found it hard to pull our legs out. During the first few hours of the journey some of the prisoners began to falter. In order to keep up the tempo of the march, the guards nearest to them kept setting the dogs on them, or else prodding them with their gun butts, interspersing this goading with harsh laughter and Russian curses. The hardier prisoners tried to help the weaker ones along, but even they soon began to find the strain too much for them. Finally the whole column was ordered to halt and we were allowed to sit down on the road for a short rest, since even the guards were very tired.

We travelled thus for a whole day and evening, with short intervals of rest. Unfit for such marches because of our long immobile life in prison, we were both hungry and deathly fatigued, when we saw the reflection of some lights in the distance. It was about twelve o'clock at night when we arrived at Camp Palkino. Our numbers were checked and we were then marched through the gates of the wire enclosure. We were so exhausted that even the dirty barracks semed like home. We didn't mind the cold or the bed-bugs any more, and we fell into a dead slumber.

On the next day we were called for medical inspection, if such it could be called, for it was a mere test to see if our muscles were in fit condition for hard labour. The inspectors looked us over like a herd of cattle, and jotted down remarks in their notebooks. Whenever someone tried to complain of sickness, the inspectors would merely laugh in his face.

"Never mind, you won't die. What do you think you came here for, to dance at a ball?"

Eight hundred men were taken out of our contingent, and the rest were housed in groups in those barracks which had been vacated by a former contingent. They worked in the forest, or at the giant saw-mill, a quarter of a mile from the camp on the bank of the River Lozva. In the spring, millions of board feet of logs were floated down this river, and the saw-mill was always kept in operation by the three thousand prisoners who worked there, toiling in twelve-hour shifts. A branch railway was built to this mill from a main line, and trains carrying lumber and building materials rumbled over it incessantly.

We met people at Palkino who had seen many slave camps in Siberia; but they considered Palkino one of the best, because the work here was less onerous and the place was lighted with electricity. Otherwise conditions were much the same as elsewhere.

Not far from the camp, on the other side of the wire enclosure, we saw a high log palisade. It looked very much like the enclosure around a Muscovite village of the time of Ivan the Terrible. No one knew what was behind this palisade; but one of the older prisoners said it was a *kartser*. Any prisoner found breaking the rules, or failing to follow the instructions given to him, was sent to this prison within a prison for a few days. It was unheated. If his offence was of a serious nature, he was left there in his underwear, and in some cases completely nude, with nothing to lie on but bare boards. He was given but a pound of bread and a cup of water per day. After four or five days in the *kartser*, many came out in such a weakened condition that they soon died.

In the summertime the mosquitoes took the place of the cold as a means of torture in this dungeon. They came in through a small open window, near the ceiling.

These *kartsers* were built according to an "all-Soviet standard," and they were the same in all the camps where we laboured. They were an inevitable part of every Corrective Labour Camp.

I did not remain at Palkino. The next morning we were awakened at four o'clock and ordered to dress for the contingent. Before our departure we were given some soup made from spoiled fish, a little bread, and two salted herrings. We started out on the journey in an hour along with a group of prisoners who had been in the camp previous to our arrival there. For about twelve miles we travelled over a corduroy road laid over muddy ground, built with logs the size of telegraph poles. These logs lay side by side, reinforced by large iron braces. This road had been built somewhat earlier, about the time the Ivdel project was being constructed. Logs were hauled along this road for building purposes. So were materials and machines for the construction of the huge saw-mill at Palkino. This road was built without the aid of machinery. Many thousands of prisoners used nothing but their hands to finish it and many died before it was completed.

In a clearing among the trees we noticed mounds of snow on level spaces. This made us wonder. Some of our fellow workers told us that these were graves with piles of earth on them, which the snow had covered. This particular spot was one of eternal cold. Here even in summer the ground never thaws more than a yard below the surface. A hole is dug big enough to hold three to five hundred people. Corpses are brought ten or fifteen at a time until the hole is filled, and then it is covered over with clods of frozen earth to prevent any stench in the summertime.

Sometimes the wolves paw through this earth and devour as many of the corpses as they can get at. When this happens a few men are sent to cover up the grave again.

I looked at those unmarked graves and wondered if per chance my old father might not be buried in one of them; for after his arrest no one knew where he had disappeared. His only crime was that before the revolution he had possessed twenty-five acres of land, and afterwards, had persistently adhered to his religious beliefs, despite Communist persecution. In 1938 he and a few others had renovated a stable for worship. For two Sundays an old priest held mass in this place. On the third Sunday two NKVD trucks came to this church and arrested everyone present. Their faith was their only crime, for which they suffered an unknown death either

in these or other graves, without a cross or burial service
to mark their last resting-place.

We saw dozens of similar graves all over the *taiga*,
near the slave camps. And the Lord only knows how
many more of them there were scattered over Siberia,
in the frozen North.

Before dawn we came across a large village at the end
of the Ivdel Highway. There were about four or five
hundred log buildings laid out on both sides of the Ivdel
River. This village of Ivdel had been constructed recently by slave labour on a cleared site in the forest. In
the centre of the village there stood on a hillock a large
two-storey building with a colonnade of two hundred
year old pine logs along the façade. On a large sign
several yards long were the words: Headquarters of the
Ivdel Labour Corrective Camp of the NKVD, USSR.

Behind these walls reigned a Muscovite suzerain, holding power of life and death over thousands of people.
This gloomy structural monstrosity with its great colonnade looked more like a giant octopus, with its tentacles
extended all over the *taiga* to the slave camps, sucking
out the last vestiges of strength from those unfortunates
who were wasting away in the forests.

On the map of the innumerable concentration camps
of the USSR, Ivdel was marked with the smallest dot,
for at that time this camp had under its jurisdiction only
three hundred and fifty thousand slaves. Others had as
many as two million.

There is no doubt that in the years 1939 and 1940

there were about fifteen million prisoners in the concentration camps where slaves worked from day to day at little expense to the state, enhancing the construction of the prison of nations, and helping to supply funds for Communist military might, intrigue and espionage abroad. This army of slaves must have been greatly increased since the "liberation" of many other countries. Former prisoners of the Hitler camps were also sent to these camps. After the Second World War they came back to the "Fatherland" of their own free will; but when they got there they were not allowed to mix freely with the population for fear they might spread stories about the better life outside the USSR. This outside world must be painted in the darkest colours!

We passed Ivdel in a quick march, and then were swallowed up again by the *taiga*. Here and there around Ivdel the same type of mounds could be seen, covered with snow, but there were no crosses or signs to mark the graves of those who had built that cursed village. There were many mounds on all sides of Ivdel, something of which that place is doubtless proud.

Beyond Ivdel in the forest we were given a thirty-minute rest. We sat down for a meal of bread and salted fish and snow. But the guards and the dogs gorged themselves with preserved meats.

Then we were on the march again. Soon we came to a clearing in the *taiga*. Here we met with a strange sight — eight real Ukrainian houses constructed of logs, plastered in the crevices with clay and white-washed. The only thing peculiar about them was the roofs, which were made of boards instead of the customary thatched straw. These houses were surrounded by wooden fences and porches and they had annexes for cattle. This was one of the very few pleasant surprises of our sojourn in Siberia. It reminded us so much of home! We glued our eyes upon this settlement, and we noticed that the people who were out in the yards, having spied us, immediately ran back into their houses and began to peek out at us from behind the curtains on the windows. At first we thought that life in the *taiga* had made them wild; but we learned later that they were merely following the instructions of the NKVD administration to act in this manner on the approach of any prisoners. We also learned about the origin of these people.

In the years 1929 and 1930, the period of intense collectivization in the Ukraine, many peasants were exiled into this remote part of the *taiga*, to places where human feet had never trodden before. They were literally dumped here with only enough food to last them for a few days, and a few saws and axes, as if to say: "Now you are on your own."

To protect themselves from the intense cold they hastily constructed temporary shelters. Their beds were made of twigs piled on the snow. On these they slept in their rags. It is no wonder that out of an original group of two thousand settlers, only fifty or sixty remained to finish the bunkhouses. The others were in too weak a condition to be of any use, and those who did not die numbly waited out the winter until the coming of spring. There was no way of escape. Where could they flee? How was one ever to get out of this gloomy and limitless expanse of *taiga?* And yet there were some brave souls who tried to escape; but few ever succeeded. The *taiga* took care of that.

Those who survived the terrible winter of death built houses for themselves out of the logs. They set traps to catch wild animals, and lived on berries and mushrooms. In time they domesticated some wild goats and deer, and even enticed bees into hives. We saw four such settlements as we marched through the *taiga*.

CHAPTER 15

Life in the Lumber Camps

THE NEXT DAY and through part of the night we marched about forty-five miles. Late at night, after a hard journey, we arrived at Camp Yurkino.

This camp was built on a large clearing in the forest. We noticed the silhouettes of four small log barracks as we approached. There was no light other than the lantern in the guard-house near the entrance. We waited half an hour before the gates opened and a sleepy captain of the guards came out, with two aides. With the help of the lantern they counted us and then allotted us to the various barracks, which had been completely vacated by a former contingent. Thus there was no fire in the stoves. There was no light and we all herded together like a flock of sheep looking for some place to sleep. Somebody had a match and lighted some chips found near the stove. Then someone brought in a little wood from the outside, and we made a fire in the stove. We all hunched around it to warm up a bit after such a strenuous journey in the cold; but our legs now felt too weak to hold us up, and so we all sought out a bed on the shelf-like bunks. Two were left on duty to tend to the fire, and the rest of us soon fell into a deep sleep which even the cold and the bed-bugs could not disturb.

We were soon awakened by the shrill blowing of a whistle. That we had completed a long trek two or three hours before did not matter. The camp regulations must be strictly adhered to. And so we were hustled out of bed at five o'clock in the morning.

A guard rushed into the barrack, yelling at the top of his voice, "Get up for the inspection. *Daway!*" It seemed as if no guard could give an order without the use of this damned word, *daway*, which means "give"! During the whole time I spent in prison and in Siberia I must have heard this word many thousands of times, in various combinations: "*Daway*, get up; *daway*, come out; *daway*, keep on working; *daway*, faster; always, *daway*, *daway*, *daway!*" This *daway* finally got so sickening, that its very utterance used to inflame the nerves. It seemed that if this accursed word had been taken out of the mouths of the guards, who were recruited preferably from among degenerates, it would have taken away the greater part of their vocabulary.

In a few minutes we filed into line before the barrack, and a new guard held up a lantern to check our numbers. Since he found it difficult to count two hundred and fifteen prisoners in the bitter cold, this procedure lasted more than twenty minutes. After the check-up he ordered us to stand at attention, picking out twenty of us to chop wood in the camp grounds. Tomorrow, he said, we would all have to go and work in the forest.

"The superintendent of the camp will let you rest today so that you will be able to work better when you get to the woods," he said. This humane attitude somewhat surprised us; but when two sleighs later pulled into the camp, filled with saws and axes, we realized why the chief had been so generous. Until that afternoon he did not have the equipment ready for an immediate trip to the forest.

We luxuriated the whole day on the bunks. Each of us did some work for about an hour. Twice during the day we were given some barley soup and two pounds of bread. The prisoners whose footwear was worn out were given *bakhili* and *lapti*. I had never heard the word *bakhili* before, nor have I been able to find it in any terminological dictionary. These were cotton stockings, about a foot long, lined with hemp. The *lapti* were tied with strings over these stockings. Those who had no short over-wear were given cotton jackets.

We were awakened at five o'clock the next morning. In three quarters of an hour we were supposed to wash up, eat, take our ration of bread and form ranks before the barrack. To every three men was given a long saw, called by the prisoners an accordion, and also a wooden shovel for removing snow. We were divided into four groups and sent in different directions from the camp. Each group had four guards equipped with rifles and blood-hounds.

We travelled along the road for some distance and then turned into the woods. Two guards led the way for us and the other two followed behind us. Soon we stopped at our destination, a forest of fir and cedar trees. Dawn was now starting to break.

One of the guards got up on a stump and began to yell: "Attention, everybody; listen carefully to what I have to say."

With a somewhat ridiculous show of aplomb and self-importance, he gave us a few "professional" instructions as to how we were to proceed with our work. Briefly, they were as follows: each person was to cut from 81 to 324 cubic feet, depending on the thickness of the trees. These trees were to be sawed not higher than eight inches from the ground. They were all to fall in one direction, so that it would be easier to pull them out of the woods. The branches were to be trimmed off neatly so that no knots would show, and then were to be piled up and burned. The trees were then to be sawn into three to six yard lengths, depending on their thickness. Failure to comply with these rules would be punished with a stay in the *karster*. Failure to fulfil the imposed quota of work would mean a reduction of the food quota.

"Don't try to escape," concluded the guard. "All around you is the *taiga*. Anyway, we'll catch you with the dogs, and then we'll shoot you on the spot!"

The instructions ended with these remarks. Henceforth we were supposed to be on our own. The guards allocated us in groups to various points in the forest. They themselves remained on the sidelines, picking out one of our number to carry wood and to stoke their fires for them; and there they remained until the end of the day's work.

Our group was given an extensive area of the forest to work in, and so we had ample opportunity to range the woods unnoticed. We could even have attacked and disarmed the guards, but what afterwards? What could one do in the deep snow of the expansive *taiga*, with nothing to eat but a small piece of bread? The time and the place were inopportune for escape, and everyone realized the folly of any attempt. A further deterrent was the existence of wild Siberian tribes in the *taiga*. For each escaped prisoner that was caught they received a quart of whisky, twenty-five pounds of flour, and two pounds of sugar. They had plenty of incentive for the hunt once they came upon a trail.

Some attempts at escape were made in the summertime, but they nearly always ended disastrously. When the check-up disclosed at the end of a day that a prisoner was missing, the alarm was sounded, and an armed guard with blood-hounds hurried in pursuit. All neighbouring camps and railway stations were notified by telephone to be on the lookout for the fugitive, whose description was given from a reference to a portfolio. When caught the fugitive was usually shot on the spot, or else he was beaten half to death and given an extra three-year prison term. The other prisoners were duly informed about this punishment in order to deter them from attempting the same thing. Some of the prisoners managed to escape without leaving any trail, but no one knows what finally happened to them, whether they perished in the forest or died in the *taiga* mud, which, like quick-sand, swallowed up more than one person. Or whether they actually made good their escape. It was hard to hide in the USSR, since all new arrivals came under the scrutiny of the NKVD. Even if they succeeded in their escape, it was impossible to secure employment without a passport.

At Palkino we had been told about attempts at escape. When the cars were loaded at the saw-mill, the fugitives hid among the boards, which were laid in such a way by their friends that they were able to crawl out later on. They rode thus, until nightfall, and they came out when they felt that the train was slowing down. Such an escape was a very difficult matter, since a guard was planted at the loading of every five cars. And yet four prisoners did escape in this manner. Later they informed their friends about their success. This escape was successful because the guards concentrated their search in the *taiga* instead of in the freight cars.

A subsequent attempt at escape by two prisoners in this manner had fatal results. The train which carried the fugitives was halted even before it got well started. The guards opened up the cars and put the dogs on the scent. The car in which the prisoners were hidden was brought back to its original starting place, and the guards gathered all the other prisoners together. Then in their presence they ordered the fugitives to come out of their hiding-place. They were beaten unmercifully and then thrown to the dogs. One of them died from a badly lacerated throat; the other one in a half dead condition was shot on the spot.

Paul Dmytrenko, one of the prisoners from the Kiev area, rushed at the guards, cursing them.

"You damned bandits and murderers, now you can shoot at me."

And with these words he tore his shirt open and bared his chest. Without the slightest hesitation the camp chief pulled out his revolver and with two shots killed the brave and rash young man.

For two days the fugitives lay where they were slain, so that they could be seen by the other prisoners while they were working.

Thus all attempts at escape from Palkino by way of the lumber cars were squelched. And yet one adventurous prisoner did escape that summer by hiding under the locomotive.

Now we all realized the futility of attempting to escape, and kept to our work. After our long and wearying period of inactivity in the prison we were glad at first to do physical labour. Our joy, however, was soon dissipated when we found that the work was too hard for completion of the large quota put upon us. By the noon hour we were tired, and in the evening at quitting time we were hardly able to raise our arms.

In the afternoon of the first day one of our group was hit by a branch of a falling tree. He was brought into the camp unconscious and died the next day. Accidents like this were fairly frequent, for the prisoners had heard only one "professional lecture."

Before evening the scaler measured off the fallen logs and began to figure out their cubical contents. We were disappointed for we had completed just half of our quota; this meant a decrease in our ration of bread and *balanda*. It is true that this rule was not strictly adhered to during the first week, though this was not from any humanitarian motive, but rather to preserve the prisoners for the hard work later on.

During my imprisonment in Siberia I worked at different jobs. Exclusive of the work at the saw-mills, where mostly women and the least vigorous of the men laboured, tree cutting was considered the easiest. But it actually was not.

In the *taiga*, trees are cut only in the winter. The snow is waist deep then, in some places as high as the shoulders. Cutting is hindered not only by the snow but also by thick willows and other underbrush. It is thus necessary first to clear the snow away, and then when the trunks fall, the branches are trimmed off. When the trunks are cut into pieces, they are turned and trimmed on the other side. The only tools we had to aid us were a saw, a wooden pole, an axe and a shovel.

The hardest work was in the areas where a hurricane

had passed. In the summer there are many terrific rain-storms, usually accompanied by high winds, which tear trees out of the ground by the thousands, roots and all. As the roots extend only a yard deep into the eternally frozen earth, these trees fall on one another in several layers; but the work of cutting them must go on at the same old quota.

I have already spoken about the quota. In order to ful-fil it, one had to labour all day long until "the seventh sweat" almost without rest. I worked without an overcoat in a woollen shirt I had brought with me, at fifty below zero, but I did not feel the cold. During the short rest periods I went over to the fire to warm up a bit and rest. We had to work hard and fast to fulfil the quota, since it was a matter of life and death. Those who reached the quota got two pounds of bread and two servings of *balanda*, and sometimes three or four herrings. Those who fell below the quota received proportionately less bread and only second grade *balanda*.

The Stakhanovite Shockworkers, who went as high as one hundred and fifty per cent of the quota, received two and a half pounds of bread and special *balanda* in which there was an occasional frozen potato or two. Under such conditions of diet it is no wonder that everybody tried his hardest to fulfil the quota. Those who failed to do so found their health soon waning from lack of food. For these weaklings there was only one end — the grave. The administration showed no sentiment in these matters. All they were interested in was a high standard of productivity per person. What did a few dead prisoners matter?

Later on we had to exert ourselves more than ever in pulling out trees onto the icy road and then piling them up on the river bank.

While we were labouring in the forest, another group of prisoners was preparing an ice road to the river, very wide and about a mile long. They levelled it off with snow. Later on they hauled huge loaded sleighs with wide runners along it. The ruts made by the runners were partly filled with water so that they soon had an ice railway laid out. Putting on harness, like the vagabonds of Répin's famous painting, we hauled many thousands of cubic yards of logs over this road to the river on these massive sleighs.

Such ice roads led to the river from other labour centres. Before the start of the spring log drive great piles of logs lined the river bank for several miles. They were sorted according to thickness.

As soon as the ice in the river began to break up most of the prisoners were called in for the drive. They rolled the logs into the water. All along the river there were brigades of workmen under guard, whose duty it was to stop the logs from damming up the river. Some of the logs were caught in the booms near the saw-mill and taken out for use in that place; but the rest of the logs floated farther on, perhaps down to the railway lines.

Logs were cheap, for the prisoners who fulfilled their

quotas were paid only from four to ten rubles a month. They received this money only when they were freed from the camp. And since only a few out of the many millions were ever thus discharged, most of the money remained in the pockets of the state. Only the Shock-workers, who fulfilled two hundred per cent of their quota, and who earned twenty-five rubles a month, were allowed to send home fifty rubles every few months. This was mostly for propaganda purposes, as if to say: "You see, they're sending money from Siberia. It looks like they're pretty well off there."

But we ordinary labourers were only allowed to take out on account two or three rubles to buy a package of *makhorka* and some matches. In reality our entire monthly wage was less than the price of two pounds of sugar, which in any case could not be purchased as we never saw any during our whole stay in Siberia.

Siberian lumber was cheap; and the government could afford to ship it to the world markets at dumping prices. But nobody outside the USSR ever knew the tragedy of millions of slaves, wasting away in gloomy inhospitable forests, which this dumped lumber represented.

When the floating of the logs was finished, a few brigades from every camp along the river banks were despatched to retrieve the stray logs. This was most difficult work, for the logs were covered with slippery river silt; and it was hard to either pull or roll them out. Then again one could not work without gloves and a mosquito net, for clouds of these pests buzzed about us continually. We found it hard to breathe in the midst of this highly exhausting exertion. And to top it all the guards would not let us rest, for their minds were fixed on the bonus they expected to get for speeding up production.

Early in February of the year 1940 two hundred of us were transferred from Yurkino to another camp called Tansha. At that time this was one of the remote Ivdel camps, hidden away back in the *taiga*. Tansha had no barracks. Instead there were large tents on raised wooden foundations. We had to spend an intensely cold winter in these monstrosities. In the middle of each tent there was a small iron stove. We fired it until it got red-hot, but we could not warm the place. The canvas walls were still covered with hoar-frost.

We were given one ragged blanket each. For two months we had to sleep with all our clothes on, and we were always chilled to the bone. Many of the prisoners contracted lung trouble and rheumatism as well. The seriously sick were hauled on sleighs to the "hospital" at Camp Prystan. Usually that was the last we ever heard of them. It is safe to assume that they were buried in the graves which we noticed later by the roadside.

When the spring thaws came in April a proclamation from the Ivdel Camp Chief was read to us which stated that prisoners were to work only in the camp grounds in fifty below zero weather. For this benevolence we returned him some silent curses, but these would not bother him. He was too comfortably ensconced in his warm quarters to be concerned about the rest of us, half frozen and half dead from over-work, seemingly forgotten by God and man.

It was a most distressing sight to see those scare-crows of prisoners trudging back from work with heavy feet and bowed heads, dirty, tattered and deathly pale, a dull, grey and beggarly looking mass of hopeless human beings. They were a grotesque group of individuals, much alike in their degraded mien, walking more like robots than men. Under these terrible conditions of slave labour many thousands of people of high cultural standing lost their individuality, their hope for the future, and all semblance of normal human beings. All they could look forward to, and this was a wretched thing at best, was to be able to drag themselves back from work and warm their damp, rheumatic feet, eat a little *balanda*, and try to forget themselves in fitful sleep on the dirty bunks.

Actual freedom was impossible, and dreaming of it in the abstract was too distressing, so we forgot about it completely. Our souls were empty voids, for there was no end to this grey uniformity, the unbearable monotony of this beastly life. We were silent slaves with desolate souls. We neither smiled nor sang, except once in a while when a prisoner from Poltava would break into the melancholy song: "The Cossacks weep in Turkish bondage."

In the spring we were hit by another misfortune. Because of the lack of vitamins, many prisoners became ill with scurvy. At first our gums began to bleed, then our teeth began to fall out, then our muscles started to rot, especially around the joints. Fortunately during the first spring most of us got over this dread disease, while it was in its earlier stages. The following winter they soaked fir needles in barrels filled with warm water, and before entering the dining-room each prisoner drank a cupful of this bitter concoction. But since some of them refused to drink it, this medicine was mixed with the *balanda*, giving it a highly unpalatable taste. We all had to eat this meal whether we liked it or not, even though a pig would have turned away from it in disgust. Who were we to be fussy about food; and hungry people have to eat!

Because of the lack of fats many of the prisoners contracted "chicken blindness," that is, after twilight they could not see anything, and so they had to be led around like blind people.

In the spring of 1940, when tree-cutting work ended, I was included in a group which was transferred to Palkino. There we were put to work tending the drive, the embanked logs and the jams. We pulled out logs to feed the saw-mill. Then we loaded the lumber on the cars. The work was hard and the food was bad, although the barracks were warmer and roomier, and had electric lights. At Yurkino and Tansha the only light we had came from the stove, and in an emergency we used dried wood chips. Only in the dining hall a lantern flickered dimly.

Palkino had another advantage over the other Ivdel camps, in that the prisoners who filled their quota regularly were allowed to write home once a month. The letters, of course, were carefully censored. I worked my hardest, and finally was given a chance.

Words cannot picture the emotions that took possession of me when I received an answer to my first letter. I hid the letter under my shirt and sought out a spot in the camp where I could read it undisturbed. My hands trembled, and the unrestrained tears which fell from my eyes dropped on the lines written by my mother's hand in my own native land.

I preserved this letter as a most precious treasure, and reread it hundreds of times. When the depressing atmosphere of the camp got too unbearable I betook myself again to a quiet corner and read the priceless words. They were replete with the holiest of mother love and concern. It made me feel lighter at heart, and some deep spark of life began to flicker afresh within me.

In conclusion my mother related how she was trying to secure my release, and how she was praying to St. Nicholas for success. I could read between the lines of her letter that she thought that her efforts would be futile, but she did not say that in so many words. She assured me that everything was all right at home, and told me not to worry about her. In turn, I wrote that I was back at my old profession; that I lived in good quarters; and that I lacked for nothing.

In the outside "free" world people learned how to

write and read such letters. They knew that life even outside of prison was not free, that they were really in a prison without barred cells, where one could not express anything that did not coincide with government propaganda.

During the whole of my stay at Palkino I received four letters from home, and these revived my moral strength and enabled me to endure the life of forced labour. They were the *evshan-herbs* or magic plants, which filled me with painful nostalgia.

CHAPTER 16

Twenty Minutes from Prison

IN THE FALL OF 1940 there came to the Siberian concentration camps many new prisoners, chiefly from the industrial districts of the Urals. The old-time prisoners called them "recruits under the new Stalin law" since they had been sentenced to the Siberian camps for coming late to work. The "new law" passed in June, 1940, by the Supreme Soviet Council, provided that anyone arriving late to work by twenty minutes without good reason, was to be punished either by a term in prison, or as in this case, to one year forced labour. Changing one's place of work without permission was also punishable. This decree made the margin between the limited slavery of "free" workers and the total slavery of the forced labour prisoners only twenty minutes. From the numbers we saw coming to our camp it was evident that the law was being well enforced. It was meant ostensibly to cure tardiness, but its real purpose was to expand the forced-labour population.

Among the fresh victims of Stalin's new law were

some Red Army men who had fought on the Finnish Front. For them, as for the other prisoners, work as such was not terrifying; they had experienced plenty of that in the free world.

Among the older men were some from the worker's *élite*, who had helped make the revolution. Now they were receiving their reward. They softly cursed the Stalin constitution for introducing this new labour law and for bringing things to such a pass that people who had been doing everything in their power to build up Soviet industry now had to suffer the degradation of a slave camp for coming twenty minutes late to work. They worried most over the fate of their families, who were left back home in dire straits, since they were now considered close relatives of "enemies of the socialist system."

For the Red Army men this was quite a lesson in history. Enduring intense cold on the Finnish Front they had been defending 200,000,000 people of the USSR by order of Stalin against the "threat of imperialistic Finland." Unused to fighting in deep forest snows in the bitter cold, without adequate food or clothing, many thousands of these men suffered severe frost-bite around the hands, feet and faces. Many more thousands were killed by the Finns, who manoeuvred expertly on skis and for months held back a hundred-fold greater number of Soviet divisions.

"At that time the papers wrote," Semen Bondarenko related to me, "that 'Only the armies of the Leningrad

military district were fighting on the Finnish front.'
But in reality these troops were only a small part of the
forces that were mustered from all over the USSR.

"How many regiments of Ukrainian solders were destroyed on the Mannerheim Line was hard to determine.
I was under the impression that the Ukrainians were sent
there to bear the brunt of the fighting. Behind them
marched the special 'retreat-blocking' troops, composed
chiefly of NKVD men, whose duty it was to cut off any
retreating soldiers and to mow them down with machine-
guns, if necessary.

"In one battle our group was suddenly surrounded by
some Finns on skis and we were captured. Although our
captivity was not an easy thing to endure, we nevertheless discovered that our enemies, the Finns, treated
us more humanely than our own political commissars.

"When the war ended we revelled in the thought that
we would now be sent home to our native land and get
leave to see our families again. Instead of that we were
taken out of the camps under NKVD guard and sent to
Petrozavodsk. There about 100,000 of us were hauled
up before the military courts, which lasted only a few
minutes. We were asked where, how and under what
circumstances our capture took place.

"Out of every hundred men only five were freed. The
rest were taken out into the forest at night and either
shot down by the 'fatherland's' machine-guns or sent to
forced labour camps for ten to fifteen years. This was
our reward for risking our lives for the Socialistic Father-

land. Oh, how I would like to see the whole damned structure destroyed!"

In the same way the Fatherland treated those Red Army men and civilians who voluntarily returned home from Hitler's death camps after the conclusion of the Second World War.

Semen Bondarenko was not fated to live long. He was not the type to stand insults and persecution. For openly cursing an NKVD tormentor he was given five days in the *kartser* clad only in his under-clothing. On the fourth day he was transferred to the camp "hospital" with a very serious case of double pneumonia, to which the poor fellow soon succumbed.

Somewhere, thousands of miles away, in the Ukraine, were his bereaved wife and two orphaned children. Nobody would care or provide for them now, for the husband and father had been marked as a "traitor to his country."

At the beginning of winter of the year 1940 new prisoners arrived in our camp from the "liberated lands" of Western Ukraine and Poland. They were from various walks of life and of diverse social standing. For the most part, they were peasants and small officials, who, as usual, were charged with Ukrainian or Polish nationalism, and were thus considered "enemies of the people." This mark was employed universally. It could easily be stamped on anyone, however innocent. This was one method the USSR employed to recruit the slaves for the Siberian camps. But not all of them were able to live through the "preliminary stages" in prison as we had.

The great majority of these prisoners were sent directly to Siberia; and on the way other cars, loaded with their fellow-countrymen, who had already undergone the chair-leg examination in the Kiev prison, were attached to their train.

Mr. J. B., one of the Polish prisoners, told us the history of his arrest. Not long after the installation of the Soviet civil government, or to be more exact, the NKVD, a general meeting was called in his country town. It was announced there that the Stalin constitution guaranteed to every citizen of the USSR and the liberated countries the right of personal freedom, and the other democratic liberties. Those who did not wish to remain in the "liberated countries" under those conditions were to have the right of unhindered departure beyond the borders. The next day at nine o'clock a train would be waiting at the station for those who wished to depart for Germany. An unlimited quantity of clothing and personal items could be taken along, but furniture would have to be forwarded later on by their relatives or friends. All packages must have the names of the owners written on them in large letters, so that they could be easily distinguished. All documents and papers that might be useful in the evacuees' new homes must be taken along. The train would depart at two o'clock in the afternoon. For lack of available passenger cars, the departees would have to ride in cattle cars, but the journey would not be long.

When someone present suggested that the train be delayed two or three days to enable those going away to prepare themselves better for the journey, the speaker informed him that this would not be possible, since there was an urgent need for cars to ship various goods from the USSR to Poland, and that there would be no more trains for the emigrants to Germany. Even this train would not have been available, except that the Soviet Government wished to give them the opportunity to emigrate, since it did not intend to hold anybody in the country if he preferred to leave.

The next day at nine o'clock there really was a train at the station. All the cars were marked with chalk, designating the travel-route to Germany. There were a few cars at the front which were intended for carrying heavy, bulky articles.

People began to arrive on foot and by vehicle. Some, more cautious than the others, and more suspicious of the proposition, now began to feel a little more optimistic when they failed to notice any guards around, and saw the people quietly unloading their bags into the cars, receiving receipts for them, and sitting down on benches and chairs in the cars reserved for passengers.

On the railway platform there were only two officials dressed in civilian clothes in attendance. They answered all questions put to them by the prospective emigrants politely and pleasantly. Noticing this idyllic scene, the suspicious ones hurriedly ran for their valises. And many of the emigrants already seated in the cars began to wonder whether they were doing the right thing to depart beyond the boundaries.

Three more cars had to be added to the train because of lack of space. An hour late, it now started out on the journey. White handkerchiefs were waving from the station platform in farewell, and the voices of friends and relatives could be heard shouting good-byes. The train was to be accompanied by two civilians as far as the boundary line.

The train passed two stations without stopping, and then suddenly halted at a crossing in the middle of a field. As if from nowhere there arose an armed NKVD squad, which completely surrounded the train. A guard stood at the door of every car, shouting: "Examination of documents!"

The two civilians now showed their true colours. Along with two groups of armed guards they approached the end cars, commanding everybody to come out and show their documents. All the passengers were searched and their papers and valuable belongings taken away from them. Anyone trying to protest was struck on the shoulders with a rifle and brutally cursed. Every piece of baggage was taken out of the cars by the guards.

Following this "examination of documents," the people were forced back into the cars, and warned at gunpoint to maintain complete silence. The doors were closed and sealed with wire, which the guards had brought along for just such an emergency. The windows also were nailed tight. All the valises in which the passengers kept their most valuable belongings were packed into the front cars.

All this activity lasted but an hour, at least presumably so, since the passengers no longer had watches. The train then moved ahead, and after a short stop at the first railhead station, it turned aside to go back to the "most democratic country on earth," under close observation of the guards.

Later on these victims found themselves in the Lukianiwska prison at Kiev. At the Lukianiwska station the men were packed into Black Crows and thus perhaps forever separated from their wives and children.

In the prison they went through the appropriate "preliminaries," and now some of them found themselves at Palkino. The men from the train were charged with espionage in favour of Germany on the flimsy evidence that they wanted to emigrate to that country. All of them were forced to sign false testimony for which they received a ten-year sentence. Some of them disappeared without trace, which meant that they had been shot in the neck at the Rosa Luxembourg Street garage, or some other torture chamber.

Nobody knew what happened to their wives and children. When they tried to find out they were either ignored, or else received the following insulting answer:

"Your wife is working in a bawdy house."

The children were taken to an institution, where

they would be trained according to proper communistic precept. The mothers were deported to the Kazakstan steppes, where hundreds of thousands of female workers from the great prison of nations eked out a wretched existence at hard labour.

These new prisoners, who had been used to a normal life, exhibited a deplorable lack of initiative under the slave labour conditions. We did our best in extending a helping hand to these novices, in work and in advice, for we considered them brothers in misery, and we finally broke down the stony and cold hauteur with which we were regarded by some of the Polish officers.

The Ukrainian peasants from the West Ukraine, who comprised about a half of our new contingent, adapted themselves readily to the life of the camp; but, being people with a deeply ingrained sense of right and wrong, they found it extremely difficult to swallow Bolshevik hypocrisy, treachery and cruelty. They could not understand how a government could lie so flagrantly, twisting falsehood into seeming truth whenever it suited its purpose.

Mr. M. K., from Tarnopol, told me that life for Ukrainians under the Poles had been hard enough, but prevarication of the truth was never carried out with such devilish artistry as by the USSR. He gave us many examples of this lying ingenuity. We warned him as well as others about such open talk, but it did not have much effect on them.

Among other things this peasant told us of the following incident. At Tarnopol the home of Lawyer S. was confiscated because he lived too close to NKVD headquarters. He took his case up with the chief of the Tarnopol District, arguing that in the Stalin constitution it was provided that every citizen of the USSR was protected as to the inviolability of his home. In answer the Tarnopol chief replied that there also was a provision whereby a man could move his home three thousand miles to the East. The inference was obvious.

After this veiled threat, the lawyer asked no more questions. That very same day he packed two valises, and left the district. Other owners of confiscated buildings did not have the same foresight, and so actually did land in Siberia. This was another classical example that the Stalin constitution was written only for international communistic propaganda.

If this constitution were an honest document, then why were millions of the best farmers in the USSR branded with the odious name of *kulaks*, deprived of their property, the fruits of long years of unrelenting toil, and evicted from their homes with their families in the middle of winter and sent to almost certain death in Siberia?

Somewhat later, in 1943, when I was leaving the Dnieper region of the Ukraine for Volhynia and Galicia, I personally witnessed the havoc which the Stalin constitution had wreaked in those regions. To us, who were veterans of the Communist brutal regime, this was not altogether surprising. We had undergone even worse experiences during the long years we lived under it. One had to admire the indomitable will to live of the Ukrainian people against whom Moscow has continually been directing the full brunt of its terrorism.

At this same Tarnopol I later made the acquaintance of Dr. Olynyk, whose heavily scarred neck and temple bore plain evidence of bullet wounds. I asked him how he received those marks.

He told me that they were Bolshevik mementoes, delivered while the Communists were retreating from Tarnopol in 1941. The Communists rounded up about two hundred people and drove them ahead until they came to a ravine. Here they shot them down with machine-guns and automatics.

Dr. Olynyk fell on a pile of bodies, and lapsed into unconsciousness. When he revived he was lying on a litter of hay in a stable which served as a Ukrainian Underground hospital. A strange man was binding his head with a bandage, and a woman was aiding him. It was several months before Dr. Olynyk was able to rise.

He learned later that some Ukrainian insurgents had stumbled upon the dead bodies in the ravine, and that his groans had attracted their attention. He was the only one left alive.

At first they kept him hidden in the stable, since some of the Bolsheviks had stayed behind; and then he was taken to a hospital. The doctor informed him that he had had a miraculous escape, since the bullet had entered only a fraction of an inch from the vital spot in the temple. This was how he got his souvenirs from the "comrades."

Such slaughter was not restricted to Tarnopol. All over the Ukraine, the Bolsheviks liquidated thousands of innocent people on the flimsiest of suspicions. When the Soviet armies retreated from Lviw, before the German advance, the inhabitants found the bodies of more than nine thousand prisoners. Some had been tortured beyond recognition. Thousands more from the Kiev prisons had been taken out and shot in the Darnitsky Forest and the Misholovka Ravines.

Right in the heart of the city of Kharkov thousands were burned alive in the NKVD prison, and the same kind of evidence was found at Krenenchuk. At Nikipol eight hundred bodies were thrown into huge oil tanks, with the intention of setting them on fire. It is difficult to estimate the numbers of corpses left in the NKVD cellars, along the roads, and in the ravines at that time. Those prisoners who escaped this fate, only to eke out a precarious existence along with us in the inhospitable *taiga*, were perhaps more fortunate in that they were still alive and free to dream of liberty.

So far as I know there were only two cases of suicide among them. One man threw himself under the wheels of a lumber train; another hanged himself on a bunk when his turn came for looking after the bunkhouse in the absence of the others. Before taking his own life he had washed the floor and tidied up the bunkhouse.

There were many cases, however, of self-inflicted frost-bite. Completely fagged out by the onerous work, some of the prisoners would wet their hands and hold them out in the intense cold. But it was only in cases of severe frost-bite that the doctor would let them stay away from work, and the food ration still remained on the basis of work done. Resorting to this kind of subterfuge to avoid complete exhaustion was dangerous. In the first place freezing one's hands might result in amputation or rendering them useless for further work. Secondly, if it were known that the freezing was premeditated, it would mean five days in the *kartser* in semi-nakedness, almost certain death. But the administration did not care about that, since it would serve as a warning to the other prisoners. These workers must labour for the good of Moscow and help finance espionage and subversion abroad even if they were to die in the process.

Whenever anyone died in the camp, the other prisoners remarked with bitter irony that the deceased slave had failed to justify the confidence of the Soviet Government, that he had died without finishing the term assigned to him.

None of us ever attended a funeral, even when the person being buried was one of our own relatives. But there were no real funerals. The dead person was merely dragged out by the hands and feet, and thrown into a wooden shed. After dark the bodies were hauled into the woods and hurled unceremoniously into a pit. When a fellow-prisoner died at work, he was placed on a stretcher woven from the branches of trees and carried back to camp after the day's labour was ended. Any new arrival with the slightest bit of conscience must have been shocked at the sight of these shabby, cadaverous, ragged and ghost-like creatures slowly trudging back to the camp with their dead burden.

There were a couple of dozen women in the camp, with five to ten year sentences. For the most part they were the wives and daughters of "enemies of the people." Some of them worked in the kitchen, others at the sawmill, sorting lumber. They endured the hard labour as stoically as the men. They were segregated from the men both as regards work and living quarters. Their bunkhouse was fenced off from ours with barbed wire. There was no guard near the place, but the guards had access to it at all times. Any prisoner caught in the women's bunkhouse or found in the company of a woman, was punished in the *kartser*.

Nevertheless, some of the women did become pregnant. Such women were excused from work only after eight months, when they were transferred to Camp Sama, where there was accommodation for such cases. There they did some light work until the time of delivery.

The child was left with the mother for only two months. Then she was sent to some camp to do her share of work as before, and the illegitimate offspring was taken to a children's home where children were trained as traitors like Paul Morozov, who, at the age of ten, sold his own father "down the NKVD river" and won for himself the name of an exemplary child in the USSR. There they were thoroughly indoctrinated as obedient and fanatic servants of the Soviet superstate.

CHAPTER 17

My Mother's Intercession

THE LAST LETTER I received from home came in December, 1940. It had taken a month to reach me and was filled with a mother's solicitude over my fate. She said she was going to make a special trip to Moscow to intercede on my behalf. All her former efforts had ended in failure and I doubted if she would fare any better in the capital.

Later she told me the whole story of that journey. She received a little money from my sister, and borrowed some from generous friends. She then departed for Moscow late in November. She spent the night in the station waiting-room, having no one with whom to stay, no money to pay for lodging and barely enough to buy food. At three o'clock in the morning all the "inhabitants" of the waiting-room were ousted and had to seek refuge from the cold in the passage-ways of the railroad station or else at the nearest subway-station.

For days this poor, seventy-year-old mite of a granny, living on bread and a little soup, questioned people and wandered from one government department to another, looking for justice. Time and again she had to wait in line for a chance to interview some Soviet "big shot." But she received the same answer everywhere.

"Your son was justly sentenced."

The nearest to a favourable response was the stock evasion, "We will take this matter into consideration."

This routine wild-goose chase lasted three weeks.

With her money dwindling rapidly and with little strength left to withstand the pangs of hunger and the cold, she decided to attempt the forbidden: to cut across the Red Square up to the very gates of the Kremlin.

The only time the Red Square teems with humanity is on the first of May, the seventh of November, or during some other holiday parade; otherwise it is empty, especially near the Kremlin walls, the residence of Stalin and the Politbureau.

In the centre of the Square stands the Lenin mausoleum. People are allowed to pass through this shrine, to view the mummy of the Pharaoh of the Revolution — Lenin. Farther on, between the mausoleum and the Kremlin wall, there is an invisible and effective signal system, but no people. Rarely automobiles drive up to the gates, and then only with official passes and by order of the Kremlin! The Kremlin is hermetically sealed against outsiders, for within are planned the secret schemes for use at home and for the fifth column in other countries. The Kremlin does not tolerate witnesses, for it wants to appear before the world in an ultra-democratic mask so that it can hide its real object — final victory for world domination after the Stalinist pattern.

When Mother got within a few yards of the Kremlin, a guard, bearing the insignia of a lieutenant, came out to intercept her. He signalled her from afar with his hand to halt, and then took a few steps towards her.

"Where are you bound for, Granny?"

Mother told him that she wanted to see Stalin. The guard informed her that Stalin never sees anyone, and that she had better leave because no one was allowed to trespass on that part of the square, and that she was in danger of arrest.

With tears in her eyes my mother begged him, appealingly:

"Forgive me, my little dove. . . . I have thirty rubles, only let me see Stalin, please, and I'll pray to God for you."

In reply the guard merely smiled. Then he took my mother by the arm and led her away from the Kremlin.

"Even if you gave me ten thousand rubles," he said, "I wouldn't be able to do this, for no one is allowed to see Stalin."

He spoke in Ukrainian and then, reverting to Russian, he asked her, "What is it you wished to speak to Stalin about?"

Mother then related how her only son was unjustly sentenced to ten years in Siberia, how she was now left alone in the world, with no one remaining to bury her if she should die. She appealed to him to aid her in saving her only son, and that God would bless him with much good fortune and happiness, if he would do this.

The mention of God only made the guard smile, for he did not believe in any such "fiction," especially when he was among other good Communists; but somewhere deep down in his muddled soul a spark of humanity still flickered. Perhaps he also had a mother somewhere, or was it the tears of this old granny which awakened his conscience in regard to the fate of his native land? He indicated a large building at the opposite side of the square, and told her to wait for him near the entrance at ten o'clock in the morning.

"And now please hurry away from here, and don't tell anybody what I promised to do for you, since that would only hurt your case."

With that he turned back to the Kremlin gate, and Mother went to her shelter.

The next morning, long before the appointed time, she stood waiting at the entrance of the building, which housed the office of the Supreme Soviet Council of the USSR. The lieutenant came at about eleven o'clock. He greeted her curtly and told her to follow him. Signing a pass form, which he received from a guard, he then led Mother up to the first floor and told her to wait there. He returned in about half an hour, accompanied by a well-dressed young man in civilian clothes, possibly an official.

"There's the old granny," said the lieutenant, pointing to my mother. "I think you can do something for her."

Evidently the official had been informed about the matter previously. The lieutenant shook hands with him, wished my mother success and then departed. The official led Mother into one of the rooms, wrote down her name, the year of her birth, place of residence, my name, the date of my arrest, the name and location of my camp in Siberia and so on. Then he told her to wait until he called her.

He came back again around four o'clock in the afternoon, and this time took my mother along a wide, brilliantly lighted corridor into a large room, finely finished in lacquered oak. Behind a carved table, on which stood three telephones, sat a neatly dressed, middle-aged man, who was and looked the part of a high official. My mother bowed to him, and somewhat awed by the surroundings, halted in the centre of the room. Then she greeted the mighty man before her.

"How do you do, *babushka?*" he said, and scrutinized her.

"Come closer and sit down," he told her, pointing to a chair near the table.

My mother sat down diffidently, and waited for him to commence the questioning. But the official, saying nothing, left the room and entered another chamber. Five minutes later he opened the door and beckoned to Mother to come in.

Crossing the threshold, Mother saw sitting behind a table President Michael Kalinin, the head of the Supreme Soviet Council of the USSR, whom she had seen only in pictures. Taking a few steps forward, she fell on her knees and started to weep. All her pent-up feelings burst out in one gush of sobbing, brought on, no doubt, by an instinctive fear that this was the last ray of hope for my rescue.

The President came out from behind the table and helped Mother forward.

"Sit down, *babushka*, calm yourself, and tell me all about your trouble."

He asked Mother when and where I was arrested, and where I was now located. He again asked her to calm down, promising that he would help her.

"Just go home, *babushka*, and stop crying. You will soon receive good news."

This assurance almost took her breath away, and in answer she merely made the sign of the cross, causing the President to smile.

"My dear father, I shall pray to God for you day and night!"

The interview ended with the President issuing an order to his secretary to give Mother three hundred rubles for railroad expenses. Whether he was prompted by an unguarded momentary spark of conscience or whether he did it for propaganda purposes, I do not know. In any case, Mother, although she had often been treated unjustly by the Bolsheviks, kept repeating to anyone who wanted to listen, that the only just one of them all was Kalinin. She never knelt down to pray without mentioning his name.

Twelve days after she returned home, she received an official envelope from Moscow. Her hands trembled and her heart thumped as she opened it. She found a letter informing her that because of the intervention of the President, the OSO had reduced my term of imprisonment from ten years to three, making the decree retroactive. My long-suffering mother fell on her knees and wept tears of joy before an *ikon*.

I knew nothing of this event, which played such a great part in my life. Although Mother told me in letters that she intended to go to Moscow to intercede on my behalf, I never believed much in the success of this journey. Thousands of similar attempts had been made by others before, but without results, and the intercessors were often transferred to more remote places to keep them from bothering the officials. Once in a while some relative did manage to get to a high official, but it was only because the authorities thought the time was ripe for a bit of favourable propaganda.

I consider the Moscow event a decisive moment in my life, since at that time I had begun to lose strength rapidly, making it harder to do my quota of work. For in a forced labour camp it was no work, no food, and without food it was only a question of time until one was thrown into the burial pit. I still had seven long years to serve, when the miracle occurred.

CHAPTER **18**

Liberation

ONE DAY at the end of January, 1941, I returned from work in the evening, tired to death. I warmed up a little on hot *balanda*, hung up my wet leggings, wound up my legs with rags, and then, without bothering to undress, climbed up on the bunk.

About eleven o'clock at night I was awakened by the guard, who pulled me by the leg.

"The camp chief wants to see you!" he said.

Half awake, I could not make out what he told me, and so he had to repeat that I was wanted at headquarters. I rose nervously, sliding down from the bunk. The camp chief, whose name was Shishanov, was a native of Siberia. All the prisoners hated him, for he was a true slave master. He used to appear every morning in the forest to see what the men were doing.

His usual remark was, "*Daway*, come on now, a little faster! Faster, damn you!"

If he saw any fault in the work, such as a badly cut off knot or stem, he called the foreman, and pointing at the guilty party, he would strike him several times in the face, or note his name in a book, and after work he sometimes would send him to the *kartser* for two or three days.

If any of the prisoners, from force of habit formed during their days of freedom, called him "comrade chief," he answered with a blow in the face.

"What kind of a comrade am I to you?" he would say. "You are an enemy of the people."

His face wore a perpetual scowl, and that is why, amongst themselves, the prisoners called him *Burunduk*. The *burunduk* was a vicious and vile Siberian animal known to attack man at the slightest provocation. It is a member, I think, of the skunk family, though in appearance, except for its tail, it looks somewhat like a wolverine. To me it seemed the camp chief had characteristics similar to both of these animals, and now I was being called to see him.

On my way I began to review my past deeds in the Palkino camp, wondering which one of them was the reason for my forthcoming punishment. During my term at the camp there had been two cases when men were summoned at night to hear a discharge read to them. But there were more frequent occasions when men, who had been counting the days prior to their discharge, found that their prison days not only had not ended, but that their term had been extended, although the reason for the extension was never given. One can readily picture the effect of such news on a person expecting discharge. As for myself I was prepared for any adverse contingency, since I did not harbour any hope of liberation.

Crossing the threshold of the office, I noticed the chief sitting behind a table, directly under a shaded lamp with a red silk cover. He raised his head, asked me my name, and then bent over his papers. I stood stock still by the door, crumpling my cap in my hands. He ignored me for several minutes, the standard NKVD "psychological pause," calculated to upset the nerves. Then, after settling more comfortably in his chair, the chief looked up at me.

"You are quite lucky."

Taking for granted that this was one of his uncouth jokes, to which he was prone, I asked him what he meant.

"Here, read it!" he said, holding out a paper to me.

I crossed over to the table to read it. The document stated that my ten-year term of imprisonment was reduced to three years because of the intercession of the President of the Supreme Soviet Council.

I turned my gaze from the paper to the camp chief, still uncertain whether this was a cruel joke or not. His features, however, gave no indication or sign to justify my suspicion. I began to examine the paper again, and it was then that I noticed the OSO stamp at the top and a round seal at the bottom. This could not be a forgery. Slowly the realization began to seep through my hazy mind that this unbelievable fortune the camp chief hinted at was indeed a fact. The good news made me dizzy. I began to recall the contents of Mother's last letter. So this was it.

My dear mother's prayers and efforts had wrought this miracle. It had come about by the power of maternal love and sacrifice. A stream of reminiscences rushed through my mind. In my imagination I could see her coming to me, smiling radiantly, and extending her arms to embrace me.

I was rudely shocked out of this state of mind by the booming voice of the camp chief, which never had seemed so pleasant as now.

"Now, *daway*, back to the barrack and do your work well if you don't wish to be penalized and have this verdict reversed."

Nevertheless, even this accursed word *daway* seemed to have lost most of its sting in the thrill of the moment. After mumbling a few parting words, I quickly hurried from the room, back to the bunkhouse. A couple of sleepy heads rose up to ask me what the matter was. I related the whole episode to them and they took in every detail eagerly and enviously. I felt sorry for my fellow-prisoners, for only a short time ago I was in the same state of wretchedness.

There was no sleep for me that night, for I was subjected to many conflicting emotions. It was hard to believe. Instead of seven more years all that now separated me from ultimate freedom was a month and a half.

I worked mechanically all day long. My muscles went through the motions, but my mind was elsewhere. In the days that followed my emotions simmered down, but I was not yet able to concentrate on anything but the thought of freedom. I kept counting the days and the hours until the end of the term.

My fellow-prisoners were preparing their letters home, including in them their complaints to the government officials, mostly to the President. I was to mail these at the earliest opportunity. Their relatives at home had no knowledge of what the reasons for their indictments were. Inquiries at the NKVD were futile and the subject could not be mentioned in the censored correspondence. So we tried to figure out a way that I could take the letters out of the camp with me. It was a foregone conclusion that I would be searched.

We finally hit upon a scheme. The provision storehouse of the camp stood near the Ivdel road about sixty yards from the camp, since the authorities were afraid that hungry prisoners might break into the place if it were on the camp grounds. A Ukrainian from Smila, a criminal prisoner, worked there and had a pass which authorized him to leave the camp grounds and to enter the storehouse without guard. We arranged for him to carry the letters and hide them in the storehouse. When I passed the storehouse he was to come out and hand them over to me unseen. This was a risky thing to do, for it might be noticed by a guard in the watch-tower, and I might be searched before or after I boarded the train. But we both disregarded the danger. We felt it was our moral duty to help our unfortunate friends.

On the eve of my discharge I was recalled by the camp chief who gave me an official paper addressed to the administration at Ivdel, asking them to issue me a passport and my discharge certificate. After receiving these documents I was to return to the camp, and then proceed to the nearest railway station.

At dawn the next day, while my friends went off to work, I was waiting near the gate. My documents were examined at the guard-house, and I was then carefully searched before I was allowed to go out through the open gate, alone. This was the first time in three years that I had ever walked about outside the wire enclosure by myself. I went along the corduroy road which I had traversed twice before but in the company of guards and police-dogs. Even now it seemed as if I were being followed, and I looked back, expecting to see a guard appear behind me.

After I had put some distance between me and the camp, I broke off a tree branch and trimmed it down into a cane, so as to fortify myself against any real or imaginary danger. Now that I was free I had no desire to fall prey to any wild animal. All the way down to Ivdel I did not see a single human being. When the administration building of the Ivdel camp came into view, I began to feel very uneasy. Suppose they should hold me there? This had happened to others. The very thought of it made my heart stop.

The guard at the entrance read my documents over and then pointed to a small building beside the larger one. Approaching the entrance I saw a sign over the door: "For discharged prisoners." The room, which was little

more than a box, four or five square yards in area, already
had four visitors. One, a political prisoner, had just completed a five year sentence. The other three were so-
called *bytovyky*, a name applied to criminal prisoners.
Strange as it may seem, the administration was more le-
niently inclined towards them than it was to us. They
were proud of the name *bytovyky*, since they considered
it gave them prestige over us, whom they kept calling
"counter-revolutionaries," *Petlurists*, or Trotsky-ites. It
did not matter that they were serving terms for murder,
robbery, and other crimes.

In some of the camps they ate with the political prisoners, but they lived separately in better barracks. They
were incorrigible sneak thieves. When there was safety in
numbers, or a predominance in physical strength, they
lost no opportunity in making life miserable for us. Of
course there were some exceptions among them too, who
were willing to share their last crust of bread with us. In
their own sphere they maintained a strict solidarity, mer-
cilessly punishing anyone who double-crossed his friends.
They contemptuously called these double-crossers *lah-
awi*, that is, dogs.

"Where did this crocodile come from?" one of them
blurted, pointing in my direction.

"From the same zoo as you!" I answered with equal
bluster.

This reply seemed to catch their fancy, for they all
burst out laughing good-naturedly, offering me a cigarette and questioning me about conditions in our camp.

The walls of the ramshackle structure in which we were waiting were smeared from top to bottom with inscriptions in prose and verse. Judging from the subject matter, often cynical but always vile, it was evident that this was the work of the *bytovyky*. Everything imaginable was written in this "visitor's book" of the Ivdel camp. Countless sketchy cartoons, with the names of the various camp chiefs inscribed beneath them, also adorned the walls. As if in mockery a blackboard was nailed on a wall with the warning: "Writing on the walls is strictly forbidden." At the bottom of this blackboard another inscription was written: "Is it not forbidden to suck blood out of people?"

We had ample opportunity to read these inscriptions during the two hours we sat there. Finally a wicket opened. Someone had made a very good job of painting on it the bust of a uniformed NKVD man with the head of a snake.

Someone yelled through the wicket: "*Daway*, come here!" We all fell into line in front of him. My turn came and I handed the paper to him.

The NKVD man read it over and then asked, "Where do you wish to go?"

I answered, "To Kiev."

Instead of giving me a reply he turned away from the wicket, yelling to somebody, "Wasia, look at this fool; he wants to leave this place for Kiev!"

Wasia poked his snout through the wicket, took a look at me, and then both of them burst into harsh and vulgar laughter. It grated on my nerves and filled me with gloom. I thought that my discharge had been cancelled.

"You will remain here today and work at your own profession like a free man with pay," he said.

I began to argue against remaining, setting out the fact that I had an old mother and a child. Finally he gave me a certificate of discharge with permission to live in some village or small town in the Ukraine. I was forbidden to reside in any capital or regional city. At my request he gave me a railroad itinerary to Bila Tserkva, west of Kiev. I selected this itinerary so that I would have an opportunity to stop at Kiev on the way for a short visit with my relatives.

I also received a document for presentation to the local militia, where I had to apply for a passport. In this document, which I was compelled to sign, I undertook to keep secret the treatment and conditions I had been forced to endure in prison and in Siberia. And I was warned by an NKVD man not to get off at any of the large cities like Moscow, Sverdlovsk, or Kiev, since I would be liable to two years' imprisonment for *NZP*, that is, unlawful residence. But I was not going to let myself be diverted by this threat from stopping over at Kiev and also at Moscow, where the sister of my best friend at the Siberian camp lived. I had made him a solemn promise to visit her and I intended to keep it.

On receiving my passport from the militia at Ivdel, I ate dinner at the local dining-room, and then set out for Palkino again. Night had fallen when I arrived at the guard-house. I was carefully searched before being allowed to enter the camp. At the barrack my friends bombarded me with questions about my brief sojourn into the free world.

The next day I prepared for the journey home. I received one hundred and twenty-six rubles for my fifteen months' forced labour in Siberia, some bread, a pound of herring, and two packages of *makhorka*. A shoemaker friend of mine had made a pair of high boots for me out of a piece of felt, with sheepskin soles. My working trousers, which were padded with cotton-wool, my shirt, my jacket, and a package of *makhorka*, I exchanged with a Polish prisoner for a fairly good overcoat. Another friend presented me with a cap, so I now at least partially resembled a European. In any case I didn't look worse than most of the USSR intelligentsia. But my face was rather pale, as if I had just got over some serious sickness. My hair had grown a little because during the last six weeks I had kept a rag bandaged around my head as if to hide some wounds. This was only a subterfuge to escape the compulsory hair-cut and to get back home with as little resemblance to a forced labourer as possible.

CHAPTER 19

The Journey Home

THUS I LAUNCHED out into the long journey homewards. I parted with my friends as if they were my blood-brothers. In the morning of the next day, after a careful search at the guard-house, I set out with a small pack on my back along the Ivdel road.

Near the storehouse, its keeper met me, holding on to the lapel of his jacket with one hand, as if he were trying to protect himself from the cold. Coming closer he seized me with his free hand as if in the act of kissing me. With his other hand he thrust a package of letters inside my coat under my arm. I embraced him warmly, and then proceeded on my way. Everything passed without a hitch just as we had planned.

Soon I came to the railway tracks which led to the Palkino saw-mill. I walked along this railroad almost twenty miles until I came to the nearest station, through which a branch line ran.

I reached this lonely *taiga* station in the evening. Only a few railway workers lived at the place. From them I learned that the train was not due until nearly noon the next day. I got permission to sleep on the wooden bench in the small waiting-room. I gathered some dry kindling in the woods, started a fire in the small iron stove, waited until it got red-hot, and then lay down to sleep.

Although it was March, the weather was still about thirty-five degrees below zero. I had to get up several times during the night to refuel the stove, but each time, nevertheless, I got back into "bed" feeling like a king, such was my elation at my new-found freedom.

There was no guard at the station, but perhaps the workmen were armed. Nobody questioned me about documents, and so the thought occurred to me that under those circumstances it would have been easy for a prisoner to escape, providing that he had first been able to get out of the camp successfully. But I learned later that such was not the case.

Finally, about eleven o'clock the train pulled into the station. There were about ten freight cars and two fourth-class passengers cars. I boarded one of the latter, which was already occupied by about twenty civilians and a few uniformed camp guards, the sight of whom made me feel very uneasy.

They looked me over from head to foot, then continued on with some vulgar story, which was interspersed with loud, guttural guffawing. I modestly took a seat in a corner by a window, expecting all the while that one of them would come over and examine my documents. But I was left alone. In twenty minutes the train pulled out, and I then saw mile after mile of the silent, snow-covered *taiga* recede behind me into the distance.

Every once in a while the train would stop at one of the lonely *taiga* stations. A few passengers got off and on at each stop. There was none of the hearty banter, such as one experiences on the ordinary passenger train. The passengers sat sullenly in their seats. At one of the stations the train was boarded by a discharged prisoner like myself, Mr. F., who was on his way home after having served an eight-year term. He was extremely cadaverous in appearance, looking like a walking skeleton. He was even beyond the point where he could rejoice in his new-found freedom. We spoke in whispered tones, and the time now seemed to pass faster.

Mr. F. briefly related the incidents leading up to his imprisonment in Siberia. After the revolution, his father, who had been an officer in the Czarist army, was lucky enough to emigrate to America. He settled in Chicago, where he worked in a canning factory. He fared very well there, but there was a sentimental bond holding him to the Old Country. In the local Communist papers he read about the free and rich life, that allegedly had no counterpart anywhere else in the world. He was drawn back to the "homeland," as if by a magnet. In 1924 he was back in the city of Cherkasy, where his relatives lived and where he found work in a sugar factory. Mr. F. was then about nine years old. Although his father earned much less than in Chicago, he was nevertheless satisfied to be back home.

Four months after their return, Mr. F.'s parents were arrested by the Cherkasy NKVD, or the OGPU as it was then called. Mr. F. remained free only because at that time he was visiting with his aunt at Bobrinska. His father was shot on the charge that he was an American spy. His mother was given a ten-year sentence to be served at Kazakstan. No one knew what became of her. Mr. F. remained with his aunt.

In the year 1932, to escape from hunger, he went to Kiev, finding work there at the foundry. In the evenings he took classes dealing with metallurgy.

At the beginning of 1933, the NKVD arrested Mr. F. In order to force a confession out of him that he was an American spy of long standing, he was unmercifully beaten at the "examination." It was absurd that he could have been trained as a spy at nine years of age. He was given an eight-year sentence at forced labour in Siberia. He was at Nohayevo Bay, and then at Ivdel. Extremely emaciated, with defective lungs, and half of his teeth missing, at twenty-five he looked like a forty-year-old invalid. He was now heading for the Southern Urals, since he was not allowed to return to the Ukraine. Both of us were worrying whether we would be able to find employment with our marked passports. Our common journey took us to Sverdlovsk.

In the evening we arrived at a fairly large station. This was Sama, on the Siberian main line. As we drew closer to a platform, we noticed NKVD guards spread all about the place. Again there was that sudden pulsating throb of the heart, like that of a frightened rabbit, brought on by fear of arrest and a return to the terrible *taiga*. The train was surrounded on all sides. The passengers were driven into the station, where their documents were examined. There was no careful search of the person, however, for the concentration was mostly on those persons carrying large valises, which were thoroughly searched. Before boarding the train I had divided the package of letters into four parts, which I hid, some in my boots and some under my shirt. After examining my documents, they wanted to know what I had in my small pack. After searching it they let me go into the main station building.

There I had to present my documents again at the cashier's wicket, and I was given a ticket to Bila Tserkva. After having my fare reduced, to which I had a right as a discharged prisoner, I paid out one hundred and thirty-two rubles. The thirty rubles which my friends had collected amongst themselves for me, in addition to my wages, came in very handy now, as I otherwise would not have had enough to buy the ticket. I boarded the train about midnight. It was already loaded with passengers, and I rode as far as Sverdlovsk without making any transfers. There I waited six hours before the train pulled out for Moscow. I was interested in everything along the way, even in things that were merely casual to the ordinary passenger, but I was extremely restless at all the longer stops. It took me fourteen days and nights to complete the journey.

I finally arrived at Moscow in the afternoon of a bleak, murky day in March. Here I had to fulfil the promise which I had made to my friend. The train to Kiev was not due to leave until midnight. I did not dare try to find my way around the city during the day, for I was afraid of being stopped by some policeman, who might wish to examine my documents.

When darkness finally fell upon the city, I went to the subway entrance and rode off to the address given to me by my friend. I tried to make myself as inconspicuous as possible by feigning sickness. As I travelled on this well-lighted subway, I noticed the sympathetic gazes of some women turning my way. But these were the exceptions, for in general the people of Moscow seemed hard, cold, and inhospitable.

I found the residence of my friend's sister without much difficulty. I rang the bell, and soon the door was opened by a young and beautiful lady who asked in Russian what I wanted. I asked her whether this was the place where Mrs. Z. lived, informing her that I had something to tell her. Unlatching the chain, she invited me somewhat suspiciously to come into the vestibule. I told her that I had just returned from a forced labour camp, and handed her the letter from her brother. She looked at the envelope, and still holding the letter in her hand, she rushed over to me, and kissed me in evident gratitude. I felt somewhat nonplussed, not expecting such a demonstration!

Without unsealing the letter, she took me by the hand,

led me into a room, helped me take off my coat, and then started to read the message. Tears began to flow down her face. She read and re-read the letter, wholly oblivious to my presence. I began to play with her two children. It was such a long time since I had enjoyed the company of little ones, that the very sight of them made the tears well up in my eyes. It evoked memories of the time when I used to play with my own little boy in the warm sands near the Dnieper River.

After reading the letter three or four times, Mrs. Z. sat down by my side and began questioning me about her brother and conditions of life in Siberia. There was no doubt of the great affection she had for him. The conversation now was all in the Ukrainian language, for she was an Ukrainian, though her husband was a Russian. They had met and were married in Kiev. He was a member of the Communist Party, was decorated, and now held a responsible position in an important government trade trust. At the time of my visit he had not yet returned from work.

Being by now thoroughly convinced of her sincerity I bared my heart of everything that happened in the Siberian concentration camps. I tried, however, to soften the prison and camp conditions, under which her brother still lived. We talked thus for about an hour. Suddenly it dawned upon her that all this conversation must have been tiring to one who had not eaten anything. So she led me to a very well arranged bathroom. A few moments later she handed me through the slightly opened door some snow-white underwear, such as I had never possessed even when I was free, as well as a first-class suit of clothes. When I started to object to this generosity, she reprimanded me with the warning that unless I dressed forthwith, she would not let me out of the place. She informed me that in the meantime she would be preparing a lunch for me.

I was so impressed with this hearty welcome and the surroundings of this home, with all its comforts, that I hardly knew whether I was dreaming or whether it was all real. I recalled our dirty bunkhouse with its regiments of bed-bugs, and the thought that I might some day be sent back to the same kind of thing again made me shudder with horror.

When I got back to the room the table was already set with various delicacies, which were available only to the select representatives of the party aristocracy. Bottles of wine and cognac stood on the table. I was dumbfounded by the spectacle.

Then the door-bell rang, and my hostess ran to open the door. They had a servant, but only during the day. My hostess returned, accompanied by her husband. He at once created the impression of being a Soviet functionary of high standing. His wife introduced me as a close friend of her brother. But when he learned that I had just come back from a concentration camp, he greeted me somewhat coldly with nothing of the enthusiasm shown by his wife. After asking me a few irrelevant questions, he went away to wash his hands. His wife excused herself and went out after him. It was quite evident that when they were alone she must have said something to him, for when he returned to the table I hardly recognized him as the same person. He was courtesy personified, trying to outdo his wife in his efforts to make me feel at home. When I remarked that I would soon have to depart for Kiev, he would not allow anything of the kind. He said he would find out what time the train would depart the next day. When I hinted something about the threat of arrest by the Moscow NKVD, Mrs. Z. confidently assured me that her husband would accompany me to the train. He agreed to his wife's proposal, but it was hard to believe that he would want to go with me to the station.

When we had finished supper and had lighted two good cigarettes, we sat down on the comfortable sofa in the front room.

"And now please tell me how and why you were sent to Siberia, and how you fared in prison and the forced labour camps. Be perfectly frank with me; no one will know what we say here, so be at ease."

His manner was so assuring that I no longer held back in fear, but told him the whole story in detail. He interrupted my remarks with certain pertinent questions, and at times I noticed a spark of fear appearing in his eyes, as if he were silently asking himself whether he would ever meet with such a fate. After getting the children to bed, Mrs. Z. joined the conversation and so, far into the night, I told them about my experiences and answered the questions that they put to me. It was about three o'clock in the morning when we retired. I sank down into the snow-white bed and soon was sound asleep. The next day around nine o'clock my hostess woke me up. She removed my felt boots, and left a brand new pair of tan oxfords in their place. My protests were of no avail. I quickly washed and dressed and then entered the dining-room, where my host and hostess were already seated. They gave me a small valise packed with something, refusing to listen to my protests against accepting it. My hostess gave me a parting kiss as if she were a blood sister. I kissed the two children, and in the company of my host I left this most hospitable home. I now began to feel more secure, for beside me was an important-looking man in a brilliant leather coat, with an order of the "Red Flag" on his chest. When we got to the station he excused himself for a few minutes. He soon returned, handing me a second-class ticket for Kiev. I never expected this unusual generosity, particularly since I already had my third-class ticket. I thanked him for this favour, and for his hospitality, and then we parted warmly and in all sincerity. He walked away towards the exit, and I went to the platform and boarded the train, abandoning my wretched pack at the station. In the second-class compartment where I sat there was also a Red Army major and three civilians who looked like high-ranking Soviet officials. Later on two women entered and one Turkoman. They all spoke in Russian. I took no part in the conversation, but sat quietly, reading a paper. They frequently glanced in my direction, thinking perhaps that my reticence was due to some recent illness, for none of them could have guessed that one so well dressed and travelling second class was a recently discharged person coming back from a Siberian concentration camp. When I opened my valise they were greatly surprised to see what I had in it. My own surprise was no less than theirs, for in it was the finest assortment of Muscovite *gastronom*, from appetizing caviar to delicious chocolates; yes, even a sealed bottle of cognac with a five star label on it, and also a small whisky glass. At the bottom I found an envelope, containing two hundred rubles.

The major, in particular, was ogling my valise with more than ordinary interest. The possession of these delicacies gave me great prestige. I ate with great relish, inviting the major to join me. He needed no coaxing. After drinking a few glasses of cognac together we struck up a conversation. He wanted to know where I came from and what my destination was. I told him that I had been studying in Moscow, that I had contracted typhoid fever and by permission was now going back home to my family to recuperate after a long illness. To avoid suspicion, I added that my valise had been packed for me by my cousin who worked in a restaurant in Moscow.

"Do you know," said the major, "that when I looked at you, I at once concluded that you must have gone through some serious illness."

I did not attempt to enter into any profound conversation, since during my three years of isolated life in prison and in Siberia I had lost track of what was going on in the outside world, and any ignorance on my part as regards current events might arouse suspicion as to my real identity.

At an intermediate station I sent a telegram to my mother in which I informed her of the time of my arrival. When we finally entered my native Ukraine I kept looking through the window, watching the villages as the train passed. They were still very dear to me, although many of them had been terribly devastated during the period of collectivization. Many things which had lain dormant for years now deluged my mind, forcing recollections, some happy and some sad, of bygone days.

I began to get more excited as the train drew nearer to Kiev. I conjured up a picture of what I thought the meeting with my family would be like, but somehow the vision was not plain or well-defined. When we finally reached the Dnieper bridge, and the wide silvery expanse of the river could be seen, and beyond it the Holy Lavra monastery on the hill, my excitement knew no bounds. I could not keep still. I thought of taking a short walk, but there was not enough space. So I merely sat there, nervously rubbing my palms and pressing my temples, and trying hard to repress an irresistible urge to cry.

At last we arrived at the Kiev station! I never turned my eyes for a moment from the window. And when the train finally came to a stop, I noticed my mother and sister on the platform, waiting for me. They gazed searchingly at one and then another window. Finally they spied me looking out at them. I waved my hand in recognition, and they waved back. Then I made for the exit. I cannot describe the rapture of our reunion, as we embraced each other with tears of joy flowing down our faces, and our hearts overflowing with thanksgiving. My mother kept patting me with her thin trembling hand as if to make sure that this indeed was her beloved son.

"But where is my wife? Where is my son? What has happened to them?"

My mother replied, "Nothing, everything is fine. . . . But they had to leave Kiev. . . . We will tell you all about it later . . ."

It was unwise to remain on the platform until everybody else had departed, since we might become the target of the railway NKVD. We therefore mingled with whatever passengers were still at the station and made our way out of the exit to the square outside. My mother held on to me meanwhile, as if she were afraid I would be taken away from her again.

I mentioned to them the threat of illegal residence. So we finally decided that I should stay with some close friends for those two or three days, some distance from where my mother and sister lived. I was known to too many inhabitants of their apartment building for safety, and the janitor or caretaker, who was most likely a *seksot*, or some other resident might inform the NKVD of my arrival, and that would put me in a very difficult position.

My friends gladly took me in, and my mother remained with me, as she would not let me out of her sight for a moment. In the evening my sister went home, but in the morning she was with us again. They all settled down to listen to the recital of my three years in prison and in Siberia.

Then for the first time I learned the painful truth about my wife and son. A few days after my arrest my wife received several summonses at night from the NKVD for questioning. She was advised to write a "confession" to my "counter-revolutionary" work. When she declined, saying that she refused to believe that I was guilty of such action, she was told to divorce me and have this action published in the newspapers. She was threatened with the loss of her position and banishment from Kiev if she failed to do so. Under the terrific strain my wife obtained the divorce and advertised in the newspapers that she was renouncing me. Two months later she remarried.

It was not long, however, before she was again called out by the NKVD and this time, without explanation, ordered to leave Kiev and forbidden residence in the larger cities of the Ukraine. Undoubtedly this was in retaliation for her refusal to write the "confession." Her husband and my child left Kiev with her.

I cannot describe the shock and pain that this news caused me. I knew I could do nothing but bury my sorrow deep inside my soul and try to forget.

After the feeling of joy and sorrow of our first meeting had subsided a little, I began to worry about finding work. Anyone who returned from Siberia, after serving time for some political crime, received a "wolf" passport, which specified that the holder was a discharged prisoner. When a person looking for work presented such a passport, he was usually told that there were no vacancies at the moment, although in fact there was a great need for men with technical experience. These were the directions from the central office, in spite of the fact that the newspapers had been announcing that all discharged prisoners would be recognized as respectable, full-fledged citizens of the USSR. A person with the highest educational or technical qualifications had to be satisfied with the job of assistant accountant, night watchman, courier, or some other inferior grade of work. But I was aided by a lucky turn of events.

On the third day of my stay in Kiev I began to prepare for my departure to Bila Tserkva. It was a clear, beautiful day in spring. In the afternoon my mother and I went out into the square to enjoy the glorious sunshine. My attention was drawn to a well-dressed man carrying a leather briefcase, who seemed to be approaching us. In appearance he looked like a high-ranking official. His face seemed familiar, and when he came closer I recognized him immediately. Up until the time of my arrest, he had been an important member of a Communist youth organization. He had worked as my assistant in the faculty of Engineering in Kiev University, but he had often shown a serious lack of technical knowledge. The other students, noticing this, sometimes led him into difficulties, and they frequently complained to me about his deficiencies. But I always tried to help him out, and even coached him in his studies. I suppose this is why D.K. was so well disposed towards me. Actually, he was not a bad sort of fellow at all.

But at the moment I did not know what his inclinations were, or what sort of a change he might have gone through in the meantime, and so I turned my gaze away from him and bent my head down to avoid recognition, for it was too late to retreat.

Even before he got close to us I heard him say, "Ah, Comrade Prychodko, what wind blew you back to Kiev again?"

He shook me warmly by the hand, gazing at me intently.

"My, how you've changed; life evidently wasn't easy over there!"

Being unwilling to show any sign of displeasure at this meeting, I reciprocated by shaking hands just as joyously. I introduced him to my mother and invited him to sit down with us. Looking around casually, he took a seat beside us, offering me a fine cigarette. Sizing up the situation, I told him that my arrest was an ordinary misunderstanding, and that I intended to sue my maligners now that I had been rehabilitated. I added further that when I had been passing through Moscow I had stopped off at the *Narkomat*, where they had offered me work at my old profession in one of the large Russian cities. I had refused to take up the offer because I wanted to work in the Ukraine. I said that I had two offers in Kiev, but on second thought I had decided that it would be better if I found a job somewhere in a smaller town, where I could rest up and get away from my recent unpleasant experiences.

I could see that he believed what I told him.

"Do you know what," he said, after reflecting a little, "your idea about going into the province is a good one. I think I can help you. I'll find a place for you in one of our technical schools."

He informed me that he had become a member of the Communist party, and was now in charge of the personnel division of one of the Ukrainian Government departments.

"Come to me tomorrow at ten o'clock," he said, "and I'll give you your instructions, and money for your transportation. You'll be all right there."

My heart bounded with joy at this prospect, but outwardly I tried to suppress any visible sign of gladness. So I answered him as casually as possible.

"Good. I'll think over your proposition and perhaps I'll accept it, but only on condition that later I be allowed to return to work in Kiev."

"Fine," he said, "whenever you're ready I'll help you to settle in Kiev, for we have both intermediate and higher institutions in this city also. So you had better think it over, and tomorrow I'll be waiting for you."

With these parting words he shook hands with us in comradely fashion and departed.

This fortunate incident seemed unbelievable, and like

a small boy I felt like leaping in the air out of sheer joy. With full knowledge of my predicament, my mother crossed herself, saying, "Glory be to the Lord, that we happened to be in the square!"

The next day at ten o'clock I kept my appointment at the office of my friend. Besides myself there were several others in the waiting room. In a few minutes D.K. appeared, and when he saw me he immediately asked me to come into his office. After asking me how I had slept and handing me a cigarette, he led me over to a map on the wall, pointing to the cities where there were still some vacancies. I picked out a small town on the Dnieper River. Ringing a bell, D.K. called his secretary, dictated a letter concerning my appointment, and then I parted from my new benefactor. I now had in my pocket an appointment by the Department and two hundred rubles given to me for expenses.

Before I left, D.K. said, "In any event when you get there, tell them that your case was settled by the Commissar himself and that you spoke to him in person."

CHAPTER 20

The New Job

THE NEXT DAY my sister and mother accompanied me to the station, but this time we parted in a much more jovial mood. The train pulled out and I felt quite elated, now that my worries about a job were over. In the evening we came to the small district town on the Dnieper which was my destination. I spent the night in a wretched ramshackle building bearing the high-toned name of "Grand Hotel." The next morning I readily located the technical school where I was to work, and then found the director to whom I presented my appointment. He read it over and then asked me where I had worked previously. I told him frankly that I had just returned from Siberia, for in any case that was the precise information in my passport. He immediately lapsed into an attitude of cold, scowling detachment, questioning me about my arrest. I repeated all the details regarding that "misunderstanding," my "meetings" with the *Narkoms* in Moscow and Kiev, and the pending lawsuit. This explanation, and of course the official *Narkom* appointment, evidently satisfied this party member, for he relaxed somewhat. He parted quite courteously with me, telling me to get in touch the next day with the chief of the educational branch in regard to the curriculum and the allocation of lectures. When I asked him about lodging he promised to find me a room in the school residence. With everything settled, I went out to look over the school garages and machine shops, and then to see something of the town.

It was a bright, sunny day in spring. The buds on the trees in the small town square were just beginning to turn a bright rich green; and farther down the shore, the spring waters of the Dnieper overflowed its banks. The scene had always been charming enough before my arrest, but now that I had been rehabilitated, it seemed even more attractive.

It was still hard to believe that everything had gone so smoothly for me. At times I even forgot the fact that I had been eternally branded. Whenever that odious thought began to seep into my mind, I tried to brush it away, or to convince myself that such was not the case. Meanwhile I roved about the Dnieper bank, chanting Ukrainian songs. I was stirred to the very depths of my soul by this freedom of movement near the Dnieper. Only one who has spent much time in bondage can appreciate this sentiment. I had never for a moment forgotten my native land.

On the following day I conferred with the chief of the educational division concerning the allocation of lectures. He greeted me civilly enough, telling me that he already knew about my appointment. He told me to go to the director, who wanted to see me about something. I intuitively felt that this meeting would not be very happy, but there was no way of avoiding it.

The director asked me to sit down, informing me at the outset that my appointment could not be accepted. All at once I felt my throat drying up. I looked at him questioningly. My intuition had not deceived me.

Without waiting for me to ask the reason why, the director explained, "The local prosecutor lectures on the 'Stalin Constitution' at this school. When I told him about your appointment he said I had no right to accept you as a lecturer because you were sentenced for a political crime."

I told him that my appointment came from the *Narkomat* itself, and that they knew about my sentence, but the director said he did not wish to risk his position by assuming any responsibility in the matter.

"Take the case up with the prosecutor," he said. "If he is agreeable, then it will be all right with me. He is most likely in the lecture room now, but he will be free at recess time. His name is Kaufman."

I entered the teachers' common room and waited for the recess bell to ring. I decided to take a calm attitude, otherwise my good fortune might disappear with the winds. The lecturers, who came out of their lecture-rooms, greeted me and glanced at me curiously, for by this time they all knew where I had come from. But they did not enter into any conversation with me, because they knew that Kaufman would soon come into the room.

I recognized him as soon as he appeared in the doorway. His bloated face, ruddy jowls, bulging eyes, squat figure and huge waistline, all reminded one of a copper samovar. When he got to the table, I came forward, telling him my name and asking why he objected to my appointment as lecturer.

He measured me with his protruding eyes, and then in a grating, squeaky voice, consistent with his grotesque appearance, he answered:

"You see, comrade Prychodko, we really don't object to people discharged from labour camps working, but when it comes to lecturing, an ideological field, we have to draw the line. It seems to me that the *Narkomat* did not consider the matter seriously enough when they gave you an appointment in the lecturing branch."

And then I had to repeat the old argument all over again, how the *Narkom* had considered my case, his personal conference with me, and then my appointment and final instructions. I resorted even to veiled threats, namely, that I would visit Kiev and Moscow and bring back the final disposal of the case from the *Narkom* himself. Anyhow I did not intend to lecture on the Stalin Constitution or political economy but on the construction and use of machinery, which had nothing to do with politics.

"If that is what you think, then you are greatly mistaken," he said. "There are no non-political subjects nor can there be any here. However, I have no objections to your working as an instructor."

This was indeed a victory. Evidently my bold stand, and particularly my reference to the *Narkoms*, must have frightened this self-confident, but in reality vile and provincial party aristocrat. I furthermore gave him plenty of information about my educational work, even exaggerating a bit, for the occasion demanded it.

But this latter artifice did not have any stronger effect than my fanciful tale about the *Narkoms*, and so I concluded, "Very well, in the meantime I'll accept the position of instructor, since I haven't any immediate means of livelihood; but you'll soon be asking me to take on the job of lecturing."

I knew I was being impudent, but I couldn't change my tone, for it was calculated to create a psychological impression on this prosecutor, whose mentality was quite susceptible to that kind of thing.

I therefore boldly extended my hand to him, a manoeuvre which took him by surprise; and then, bowing to those present, I went out to see the director and also the chief of the educational division. I was to start work on the following day, giving practical demonstrations after the lectures.

I got some essential text books from the library and spent a good part of the night brushing up on matters that I had partially forgotten during the past three years. And so the next day I was to go to work!

Although my assignment was not as interesting as actual lecturing, I nevertheless went at it with all the vigour at my command, happy in the realization that my students reciprocated in kind. I had missed the company of Ukrainian youth very much when I was in prison, for I had worked among them a good deal before I was sent away. I quite frequently supplemented my demonstrations with some lecturing material to enhance their success. Thus in a short time I earned a considerable amount of respect among the students and my colleagues. Some of them used to come to me for advice or information. As a result of this confidence, and because the lecturers were over-burdened with work, I was asked to take over several lecture-hours. I agreed to do this very gladly.

The two classes assigned to me were the most backward in their lessons. More than half of the young students in the one group had come from the newly occupied Western Ukraine, seeking something better in the Stalin "heaven," while some others had evidently sought refuge here after the repressive action taken against their fathers. And here it was that I made the acquaintance of one student, Anatoli, who came from a village near Lviw. Later on he was instrumental in getting me out of a very serious situation.

I could readily see that love of their homeland was not so hidden or marred as that of the youths from the Lower Dnieper; but I was cautious, nevertheless, about expressing this observation, since some one in the group might have been planted there as a *seksot*. In order to throw sand in the eyes of any such would-be informer, I devoted considerable time to extolling the development of machine manufacture in the "Country of Invincible Socialism," which had not only caught up to but even outstripped the capitalistic countries, under the very able leadership of the great and most wise Stalin. I cannot say that I was proud of resorting to such subterfuge, but it was necessary for every lecturer, and especially for me. The fairy tale about the capitalistic countries lagging behind the USSR in all things was barefacedly spread throughout the land. The people believed the story, for the iron curtain was too thick for any kind of genuine news to percolate through it. Any lecturer or speaker failing to mention the "Great and Dear Father Stalin" was flirting with a term in prison, for he immediately became an object of suspicion.

My professional work progressed very well. I took so many pains with it, even to the extent of putting in many extra hours, that in a month and a half the students in my groups came out first in the examinations.

I spent most of my spare time either wandering along the Dnieper banks, or in the nearby forest, avoiding any large groups of people.

I had no doubt that the NKVD kept me under continual surveillance. One of my colleagues, Stepan Khitenko, by his behaviour convinced me of this fact. Whenever he was alone with me he tried to draw me into anti-Soviet conversation. In my time I had met smarter provokers than he, and so I had no difficulty in diverting his efforts. I never said anything at all about my life in prison or about Siberia, for this would have inevitably led to a visit from the NKVD. Whenever anyone questioned me about these matters I merely told him that I had been working at my old job there, or that at times it was a little depressing in the camps. I did not break off my contacts with the *seksot*, for I knew that if he went away, his place would soon be filled with another informer, perhaps a more subtle one, and I might not be able to fathom him so easily. Outside of this I kept strictly to myself. I still had considerable zest for life. I would often stand for an hour near a blossoming apple-tree, watching the bees at work, or listening to the melodious rippling of the Dnieper waves. I also kept up a correspondence with my relatives, and from time to time I wrote to my two closest friends still remaining at Palkino. But I did not supply them with my address, for I had no doubt that my mail was checked by the NKVD, and I did not wish to receive letters from Siberia.

Such was the tenor of my life. Outwardly I began to resemble other normal people, and my nerves now seemed to become more steady, for I no longer experienced the same alarming symptoms as before.

CHAPTER 21

War with Germany

THE 21ST OF JUNE, 1941, was a Sunday. About ten o'clock in the morning I visited a teacher acquaintance of mine, with whom I had an appointment to go boating on the Dnieper. We had just completed our preparations, when we heard a loud-speaker announcement which said that in half an hour Molotov, chairman of the *Radnarkom*, would have something very important to say.

Tremors of fear and foreboding went through me. My heart throbbed violently. At the time I did not anticipate a war with Germany, for only a short time ago photographs had appeared in the newspapers picturing Molotov and Ribbentrop in evident enjoyment of each other's company, accompanied by optimistic commentaries regarding "friendly" Germany. At first I thought that this announcement would deal with another "Kirov murder" or some new conflict with Japan. In any case something important was about to be broadcast, since the time was not opportune for the usual propaganda rehash. The announcement that Molotov would speak tended to whet everyone's curiosity, since his voice was only heard as a rule speaking from party conventions. I had a telepathic feeling that whatever he would have to say would in some way tie up with my re-arrest. So we cancelled the Dnieper trip in order to hear the extraordinary news.

Thirty minutes later the news was broadcast that war had commenced with Germany.

"The German fascists," the voice said, "without declaring war, have attacked the Soviet Union; but the enemy will be destroyed, and we shall be victorious."

This stupefying announcement had a double effect on me: one of joy, and one of dread. Perhaps, after all, this frightful prison of nations would finally be destroyed. But, on the other hand, this declaration of war might mean a new arrest for me and many others like myself, and the possibility of serving a fresh sentence in Siberia, or even being shot. The very thought of it made me want to get out of sight.

From the very first day of the war, however, I faced the situation squarely. My desire for flight was soon dissipated, for where could one flee? Without a document one would not be able to find work anywhere, and in my passport there was the added impediment of a "wolf" brand. Even if the objectionable features could be deleted, there still would remain the tell-tale serial numbers on my passport. I learned when I was still in prison that various categories of people received various serial numbers, and that the NKVD and militia of every city had records of the figures in these series. From these records they could tell at once to what category of socially dangerous persons you belonged. Well, one could still flee to one's relations and hide with them. But for how long? In a few days some *seksot* would get wind of it, and a report would be made to the local NKVD. This was war-time, and action would be very prompt. Some other way must be found. I might enter the army and lose myself among the millions; but branded people like myself were not allowed in the army, unless it was to dig ditches or build runways and airports.

I kept on working at my job, but plans of escape continually occupied my mind. In my surroundings I had to be very cautious, for the least false step on my part would mean certain arrest. It was impossible to secure another document, but I was aided in this direction by a fortunate incident. When the students were handed out certificates dealing with the completion of their education, I managed to slip a blank form bearing the school seal and stamp on it into my pocket. I knew that it would stand me in good stead some day. It was a criminal offence to steal it, but then this was a matter of life or death.

By the sixth day of the war, many refugees were already in full flight, travelling by train, auto and other vehicles. They were all heading for the right bank of the Dnieper. They consisted mostly of the families of high-ranking Soviet dignitaries, and many officials as well. They took with them quantities of various articles. Thousands of herds of cattle were being driven from the *Radhosps,* and also great droves of hogs and sheep. And since it was impossible to get them past the milling human crowds on the bridge, they were herded straight into the Dnieper. When they finally got to the other side of the river, they were not allowed to rest, but were driven on and on. Many thousands of these animals floated down stream with the current and were dragged out by people who lived along the banks, supplying them with such a feast as they had not enjoyed since the inauguration of the Soviet regime. All this activity took place long before the sound of artillery could be heard.

While the fighting front was still hundreds of miles away, the factories stopped work and all the technical equipment and machinery were hauled to the station for transportation farther east. Nevertheless most of it had to be abandoned to make room for those countless heroes who were fleeing pell-mell to the east along with their valises containing the wages of the workers, and perhaps crammed with other stolen cash. In front of the stores there were ever accumulating masses of people waiting their turn to buy bread.

And in the squares the loud-speakers kept blaring incessantly, pouring out fantastic news about the victories of the Red Army over the fascists, telling a fictitious tale about how a small group of Red Army men had captured a whole German tank division. How the Red Army men, Ivanov and Petrov, were decorated as heroes of the USSR for bringing in the whole staff of a German Corps. After a few days the Information Bureau ceased speaking about the gigantic victories at the front. The humbug broadcasts were toned down and limited to announcements about the "hard battles against great odds" in the vicinity of Minsk. This came at the time when the fighting front extended as far as Bila Tserkva, about two hundred miles to the east. For this reason Comrade Lozovski, the chief of the Information Bureau, outdid himself in his fictional stories and endless exhortations against the insidious activities of the spies and diversionists.

And at night heavy German bombers roared over the silvery surface of the Dnieper in the direction of Dnieprodzerzhinsk, Dniepropetrovsk, and Zaporozhe.

It was during this heroic time that the radio transmitted the speech of the frightened "Father of the Nations," Stalin.

"Dear brothers and sisters!" he began.

As he spoke to the people whom only a short time ago he had regarded as cattle, and now as cannon fodder, the click of the glass filled with *narzam* clattered against his teeth and came quite distinctly over the air. He exhorted them to perform acts of heroism and self-sacrifice in defence of the homeland. But the "brothers" voluntarily surrendered by the hundreds of thousands to the enemy, not because they were lacking in courage, but because there was nothing that they wanted to defend.

If it had not been for the billions of dollars' worth of equipment and supplies poured into the country by the Americans, and for the repression of Soviet citizens by the Germans, Stalin not only would have been unable to sit in the Kremlin, but could not have held any part of the USSR. The Kremlin was saved by the stupid, cruel and indiscriminate atrocities perpetrated by the Germans upon the people in the occupied zones. The Soviet soldier had no choice. He faced either the cold-blooded mercilessness of the Nazi war prisons, or a fight with the enemy on the field of battle. In the latter event there was at least the chance of survival.

CHAPTER 22

Plans for My Second Arrest

DURING THE FIRST DAYS of the war our school received an order from the *Narkomat* to train three hundred young women as tractor and combine drivers. The prospective students were soon found. We worked from morning until night with only a short recess at dinner-time. But I found no peace during this period of restless activity. There was always the gnawing dread, especially at night, of sudden arrest and the slave camp. I kept waking up at the slightest sound under my window. Sleep came in fitful spasms. It was the same night after night.

Two weeks later, when the work of training these drivers was finished and the school closed up for vacation, I decided that now was the time to flee. I tried to get my pay, as I had no money, but for some reason it was held back. For a week I was daily promised that I would get it the next day.

I remained alone in my room on the second floor of the students' residence. Below me lived the caretaker and his family. Every morning at dawn I gathered some provisions and went off as if I were going on a fishing trip to the Dnieper. I returned after the sun had gone down and entered the building, not from the street entrance, but by crossing a neighbouring garden at the back. I cautiously looked in the caretaker's window to see if anyone was waiting for me there. When I saw that he was alone I entered his room, asking him whether the wages had been paid out yet; and then, after chatting with him for a while, I went upstairs to my room at the head of the stairs. I locked the door between the stairway and the corridor outside my room, formulating my plan of action. If I heard anybody rapping on it I intended to slip stealthily into a corner room at the opposite end of the corridor, and then climb down a tree that grew close to the window. When I got down to the bottom I would cross the garden into the neighbouring yard. This was my plan of escape if anything suspicious took place. I kept listening, however, for footsteps under my window.

Returning from the Dnieper one evening, I looked into the caretaker's room again and saw the *seksot* Khitenko sitting there. Assuming a carefree manner, I walked in and shook hands with him. Khitenko seemed just as friendly with me.

"Where have you been, my dear friend?" he asked. "I've been waiting a whole hour for you. Why don't you come up and see me sometimes? We could go out fishing together, or something. You're a pretty hard man to find!"

Not wishing to arouse his suspicions, I told him most

cheerfully that I also wanted to see him, but that some-one had told me he had gone on a trip to Dniepropetrovsk for several days. But now we could go fishing together. I asked him to come upstairs with me and we had a few smokes together.

He did not hint anything at first, but he gradually steered the conversation to a discussion of the war situation, attempting to trap me by suggesting that the Germans would soon be in our district, and that the USSR would suffer a complete defeat. I disagreed with everything he said.

"Surely, you don't underestimate the might of the Red Army?" was my reply. "You are greatly mistaken. I have seen more than one army parade in Kiev, and I have been impressed with the incomparable might of our forces. I am convinced that the present retreat is merely a tactical manoeuvre deliberately executed in order to draw the enemy into a trap."

Failing to catch me with bait like this, he asked me about my plans for the future. I told him that I would wait for a week, and then I would go to the *Voyenkomat* and ask them to take me into the army. I reminded him that others of my age had been called, but that for some reason I had been ignored. It is true that I had spent some time in Siberia, but that was because of an unfortunate misunderstanding. If the local *Voyenkomat* turned me down, then I would appeal to Headquarters; for I intended to get into the Red Army one way or another.

I now had no doubt that he had visited me under instructions from the NKVD; for none of my ordinary acquaintances would have been foolish enough to make such brazen anti-Soviet statements every time we conversed.

When he started to question me about such things as what I did during the day, where I had been, when I returned home, whether I ever went for a walk at night, I was strengthened in my conviction that some action was being prepared against me.

By this time I was well aware of NKVD methods. I knew that Khitenko's questions were directed towards finding out where I would be when the secret police finally decided to arrest me.

I no longer had any doubt that Khitenko would present his report on the visit to the NKVD, but I showed no sign that I was aware of his intentions. So I put my arm around his waist good-naturedly and accompanied him out of the room, saying:

"Please leave the exit doors open. It is pretty stuffy at night, and I would like more fresh air. I even leave my own door open."

Our conversation evidently convinced him that I had no premonition of arrest or intention of flight.

My parting words in the corridor were that I would see him the day after tomorrow without fail, but that on the following day I would be too tired after my visit to Dniepropetrovsk to meet him the same evening.

Well, this was it. There was no use putting it off any longer, for they might come to take me away at any moment now. My visitor no doubt had been assigned to make this visit to find out if I spent my evenings at home, and to secure a plan of the building. While in prison I had learned that prior to an arrest the NKVD always sent an agent to ascertain the victim's plans, so that they would not bungle the arrest and frighten him into hiding.

This is exactly what happened, according to the information I received from the caretaker after the Germans had occupied the country. About two o'clock in the morning, two NKVD-men in cranberry-red and blue caps came to arrest me. During the following days Khitenko came also to find out where I was. The two NKVD-men warned the caretaker on pain of severe punishment not to let me know, if I ever came back, of their visit.

Certainty of arrest now lent wings to my haste. Forgotten were my back wages. As soon as my friend Khitenko had passed the corner of the building I locked the door, took the blank form out of its hiding-place between the baseboard and the wall, and filled it in as follows, using a false name:

"We hereby confirm that Nicholas Pavlenko, instructor at the N. tractor school, is authorized to go to the L. Machine Tractor Station, to take part in a harvesting campaign. The passport of Comrade Pavlenko, issued by the militia of the Dniepropetrovsk District, 3.9.1937, is now on file in the school office. You are hereby requested to give Comrade Pavlenko every possible aid in his work and to see that he is adequately accommodated with lodging and food."

With considerable success I forged the names of the director and the secretary to the attestation, for I had studied the signatures very carefully after I stole the blank form.

After finishing the attestation I stuffed a woollen shirt, some clean underwear, a can of preserves, and a tractor-combine guide book into my portfolio. I left everything else in the room as it stood. I walked along the hall into another room and threw my portfolio out the window. Then I told the caretaker that I was going out for a walk, and that tomorrow I intended to go to Dniepropetrovsk for the day. I asked him to look after my room in my absence. Then I went out into the garden, picked up my portfolio, and cautiously ventured onto the street.

I started out in the direction of the wharf, and then, after getting out of sight of the residence, I turned right, keeping to the less frequented streets. Soon I came to a wide road leading out into the Steppe. I knew that this was the way to the L. MTS, which was about twenty-five miles distant, but I had never travelled on this highway before.

The darkness did not bother me very much until I came to an important crossroad, from which three roads branched off in various directions. It was about midnight and nobody was in sight. Nothing could be heard but the occasional whistling chorus of some quails in the broad fields of grain.

The night was warm, and myriads of stars shone brilliantly in the sky. I could smell the sweet scent of buckwheat flowers as it was wafted over the air by the night winds.

Since there were no directive signs on the crossroads, I sat down on the green grass by the roadside and lit a cigarette. During the whole time of my so-called freedom, I never enjoyed it so much as at that moment. It seemed as if a heavy burden were thrown off my shoulders. Illusory as it was, I was now partaking of my new-found liberty to the full, luxuriating in the grandeur of the universe about me, and the enchanting beauty of my homeland.

I sat in this blissful state of mind for a couple of hours, hoping that the night would never end. This was an escape from reality, and I had no desire to see the light of daybreak disturbing my reverie.

Somewhere in the distance I thought I heard the squeaking of wagon-wheels. I listened intently, and after a few minutes I could see the silhouette of a horse and driver. I walked out into the middle of the road. The driver stopped his horse in sudden consternation, wondering suspiciously what I could be doing there at that time of night. Without approaching any closer to him, I told him that I had lost my way in the darkness and wanted to know what the direction to L. was. He pointed his whip handle to the left, indicating the way. I thanked him and then started off. I was still under the spell of the illusion. I felt no fatigue whatsoever, but walked along easily, completely enthralled by that exquisite feeling that can only come from a communion with the solemnity of the night, the star-studded sky overhead, and the rustling of the golden grain on the expansive steppes. My whole being was brimming with this freedom. Out of the fading memories of bygone days I recalled some songs I used to know, humming them as I walked along. The brilliant light of the morning star now began to dim, and the reddish glow of dawn began to fill the sky.

In the morning I made some further enquiries about the road from a couple of herders, who were driving their cattle into a field. It was noon when I reached L. MTS.

The director of the MTS, evidently a member of the party, after reading my document, treated me very cordially. He was glad to get a professional workman, since some of his best men at the MTS had been mobilized into the army, and he was finding it hard to execute the quota. Something in his manner suggested that there was an element of humanity in him.

"We'll find you living quarters today, and tomorrow you can start work," he said. "I'll put you in charge of two combines and a tractor. I think you'll be able to handle the job."

I assured him that it would be done to his satisfaction, and then I went to my new quarters, accompanied by one of the MTS workers.

I established myself in a small room, which was part of a peasant's home. A small window faced an apple orchard, with luxuriant green grass. The scene evoked reminiscences of my childhood days, when I used to romp about and pick up apples out of the green grass in my grandmother's orchard.

My landlady greeted me warmly. When she learned that I was a non-party man, she offered me some fresh milk and bread, urging me to eat in the true Ukrainian fashion.

"You have had a long journey," she said, "and you must be hungry. I am sorry that I haven't anything better to offer you. Life has become so hard that I feel like crying sometimes. From early morning until late at night I have to work at the *kolkhoz*, without even time off to wash a shirt clean. And look how the walls have peeled! We haven't had a chance for a whole year to whitewash them. It's a drab life. You work all day long and they feed you on a concoction made from peas. But the wheat is sent elsewhere.

"I was sick and so they laid me off for two weeks. Otherwise you wouldn't have seen me here. My husband has been out in the field since dawn."

I muttered something as if in agreement with her, but I did not express any opinions of my own, since I did not wish to start any unnecessary talk that might involve me.

"The Germans are on the march," continued my talkative landlady. "They say that they are already near Kiev. There is a rumour that they intend to dissolve the *kolkhozes* and redistribute the land. Would to God that that were true! For so long as the *kolkhozes* are in existence life will hardly be worth living. And how are they going to halt the Germans when they haven't even enough to eat? When the Red Army was here last they went from house to house asking for bread and potatoes, in spite of the fact that you see all these expansive fields of grain. Where does it all go to? It is no wonder our hungry people had to go to Moscow for bread! We exist, but we do not live; and there is no end to the work days.

"Don't tell anyone what I have been saying to you, for there are evil people in the village who would immediately carry the information to the authorities. More than one villager has been caught in the spy-web and never heard of again. They are probably spending the rest of their lives in Siberia. So please keep quiet about what I told you."

I could not help smiling at her solicitation, for it was hard to imagine how a woman of her type could keep herself quiet for long. If she noticed the smile she paid no heed to it, for she kept rattling on in the same vein.

Our conversation was interrupted by the MTS director. Hearing someone coming through the vestibule she cut her talk short. The director had come to invite me to his place for dinner. His wife greeted me very hospitably. After an appetizing meal and a glass of vodka, we talked about the work at the MTS. He finally wound up with an expression of fear that further invasion by the Germans might necessitate a flight to the East. It seemed to me that he made this observation rather casually.

And then he added, "I wonder whether they will make short shrift of all the Communists? If a person hasn't done anything wrong, then perhaps they will not harm him. But who knows what will happen? There is an old saying: 'There can't be two deaths, but one is inevitable.' Well, we'll have to wait and see."

Judging from these remarks I concluded that the MTS director was not an orthodox Communist. I did not think he was trying to provoke me into committing myself, for he had all the ear-marks of a gentleman. I never heard anything derogatory about him from the other people.

Without making any observations concerning his remarks about the Germans, I asked him what the condition of the machinery at MTS was. After I had thanked his wife for her hospitality, the director showed me around the village, indicating the path I was to follow to the machine depot out in the field about a mile away.

On the morning of the next day I stood near a tractor station in the steppe. It was actually only a shack on wheels, which also was used as a shelter from the rain. All around it was the steppe, and farther on in the distance a grove of young trees. This hut was stationed about six yards from an expansive field of wheat. Near the hut there stood on a tripod a huge cauldron in which meals were cooked for the tractor workmen. Some distance away there were three tractors, and some machinery could be seen in the field.

With the exception of a man who was puttering near a

machine, no one was present when I arrived. I walked a little closer towards him and was surprised to see my former pupil Anatoli. Recognizing me at once, he shook hands with me joyously.

"How did you get here from so far away?"

I told him that I was sent here to work at the MTS, but I was forced to admit that I had another name. I did not want to make this admission, but there was no other way out of it. I did not doubt that Anatoli was an honourable young man, but there was always the chance that he might inadvertently make a slip without intending to do so.

"I don't know how it happened that they got things mixed up," I said, "but I was sent out here under the name of Pavlenko. I didn't know this until I arrived here. I didn't want to make any change as this would have necessitated a return to where I came from, so I let the name Pavlenko stand. In any case, what does it matter? However, would you please call me Comrade Pavlenko henceforth?"

I don't know whether he had any suspicions or not, but he gladly agreed to do this.

Soon the rest of the tractor drivers began to arrive, and other machinists as well. Among them was the foreman, a candidate of the party, and the secretary of the local *komsomol* division, who also was a tractor man. They all greeted me as if I were an old acquaintance, even with familiarity. I greeted them in kind, and after a couple of days I was as much at home with them as a fish in water. That same day I began work on a caterpillar tractor with two combines.

Each evening I returned with the others to the village, and at dawn we went back to work.

Two weeks thus went by uneventfully, but there were great changes at the front. The Soviet Information Bureau now began to transmit news of the battles around Bila Tserkva; but this actually meant that Bila Tserkva was now far behind the real battle front. Rumours placed the front somewhere near Kirovograd. Every night huge German bombers were flying high in the sky, and we heard heavy explosions over the Dniepropetrovsk and Zaporozhe regions.

One day when we came to work we found a mass of leaflets scattered all over the field. They were German propaganda circulars, replete with warnings about the imminent defeat of the Soviet armies, the coming liquidation of the *kolkhozes*, and the approaching end of the Muscovite repression of the Ukrainian nation. The circulars exhorted the Red Army men to give themselves up into captivity, where human rights would be recognized, and where they would find abiding prosperity. This circular stated that it should serve as a passport enabling any prospective deserter to freely cross the German line.

Our foreman ordered us to gather the papers up and hand them over to him, since he did not want the members of the *kolkhoz* to read any of them. We naturally did not pick them all up, and so the rumours about the advancing front spread with more intensity throughout the land.

About noon of the same day the MTS director visited us. As usual, he was interested in the progress of the work and the condition of the machinery.

"Well, boys," he said, "you'll have to tighten the screw-nuts, for it will be too bad if we don't execute the plan!"

After dinner he went out into the field with the men, and soon he came to my tractor. I was doing some oiling at the time.

Bending down, he asked, "Do you know Comrade Prychodko?"

This question flustered me so much that for a moment I was dumbfounded. Putting my oil can down, I turned to him.

"What did you say?"

He looked at me intently, repeating my real name. He must have noticed how excited I was. I soon gained control over my emotions, however, and after a short pause, to collect my wits, I told him that I did not know any such person.

Without taking his searching gaze off me, he continued, "Yesterday I was at the N. MTS, looking for some supply parts. The director told me that the NKVD had been making enquiries as to whether there was a certain Comrade Prychodko from the N. tractor school at the MTS. After looking over the lists he told him that there was no one by that name. The NKVD man entered the names of all those who had started working within the past month at all the local MTS into his notebook and ordered us to inform the NKVD at once if any such person should try to secure employment. Over at N. they have already arrested over a dozen men. Are you sure that you don't know that person?"

"No, I don't," I replied. "Perhaps he worked there before I came, for my appointment was accepted only a few months ago."

There was no doubt about it. The director knew that all this talk concerned me, but he did not wish to turn me in. At the same time he was afraid to warn me openly about my danger. I drew this conclusion from the fact that he refrained from speaking about it when others were present, and that when we two were now alone he spoke to me in a whispering tone of voice to prevent the combine-wheel steerers from overhearing us.

"Well, good-bye for this time!" he said.

Straightening up, he crossed the stubble field over to the road. Having finished oiling the machine, I got up behind the wheel, gave the steerers the signal, and then moved ahead. But I could not drive the thought of imminent danger from my head. I had no doubt that the NKVD would investigate the names they had in the notebook and discover the forgery in my attestation. I was thinking so much about how to get out of this nasty situation that I drove the tractor out of line several times.

CHAPTER 23

Preparations for Flight

THE ONLY ALTERNATIVE was flight. But where was one to flee? I had heard that, because of the great number of desertions, all the roads were being blocked, and all suspicious persons arrested and handed over to the military tribunals. What chance would I have with my wolf passport? Perhaps the best thing to do would be to find refuge in the fields. But how long would I be able to stay in hiding without food? If I appeared in the village I would surely be arrested. If I could be sure that the Communists would evacuate within a few days it would be a different matter. But as yet no cannon fire could be heard even at night. There were no definite signs that the local Communists were preparing for flight. I decided in the meantime that I would not spend the nights at home.

Sometime in the afternoon the sky grew heavy with storm clouds. We unloaded the grain from the bunkers into trucks, covered the tractor with canvas, and then fled with the steerers to the wagon-hut, since it already had begun to pour. In an hour the sky began to clear, but since cutting with the combines was no longer feasible, we all went home.

Anatoli and I lagged behind the others. Twice before he had invited me to his quarters where he lived with his wife, whom he had met shortly after finishing his education. This young couple always greeted me warmly. Both of them were very critical of life in the *kolkhozes*, and of the USSR in general. I told them very little of my own personal history, as I was afraid, not so much of treachery on their part, but of some careless remark. I warned them, however, not to express such sentiments in front of others, as some people might be only too willing to report them to the authorities.

Now I wanted to establish closer contact with Anatoli in case of flight.

I said, "It seems, my dear friend, that you have not taken my advice about caution. Why? Only today you flippantly told an anti-Soviet anecdote. Some one might report you and cause your arrest."

He was surprised.

"How is that?" he said. "I didn't commit any crime."

He was still too naïve to know that one could be arrested for ordinary criticism of the government, or even for lesser reasons.

"You have to be on your guard against danger," I told him. "If you are ever threatened with immediate arrest, you should flee; for this is war-time, and you're liable to be shot forthwith without any reason. In any case I shall show you a good hiding-place tomorrow. If you should feel any foreboding of danger, go and hide; and at night I'll bring you something to eat. You can't go out seeking food yourself, since you might fall into the hands of the NKVD, directly or indirectly."

I did not wish to tell him that it was I who was actually faced with this danger, but the next day I led him to a hide-out I had found.

I had discovered this hide-out in a nearby ravine some time before. It was a small cave, washed out by the rains, so well enclosed by a growth of grass and a small blackberry bush, that no one would have noticed it even from a few feet away. But Anatoli remembered.

As soon as we reached the village, Anatoli and I parted. I went home and ate supper. After good-naturedly bandying a few words with my landlady, I lay down to rest; and when it began to get dark I left the house, telling her I was going out to a party, and that perhaps I would stay out all night.

"You must have found yourself a brunette!" she called after me.

I walked along the street in the direction of the village club house. Then I climbed over a fence, and after passing through a meadow I came to a field, through which I kept walking until I came to the tractor-hut. I decided to spend a few nights there, and afterwards I could hide among the sheaves in the field, or in some strawstack.

I never considered hiding out at Anatoli's place, because they might look for me there.

In the field, not far from the hut, there was a large straw-thatched shed. The grain which was threshed by the combines was dumped here; and when it had dried a little, it was hauled to the railway and granary. An old man was night watchman at these two buildings. In 1930 his property had been confiscated. He had fled from the village; but after the wave of state robbery and murder had subsided, he returned home. Since he was over sixty-five years of age, he was left strictly alone and was given this job.

Some distance from the hut I was met by the old man's dog. As I was no stranger to the dog, he came over to me, romping playfully all around me. He was well-trained by his master. Whenever he heard anybody approaching the shed or the hut, he would run out towards the trespasser, barking all the while. Now when danger was threatening me, I thought of this aid.

The old man and I met near the hut.

"I thought it must be one of our own men," he said, "since Zuchok did not bark. What's the matter, can't you sleep?"

I greeted him and told him that I had a touch of insomnia, that it was stuffy in the house, that the fleas were getting a little too annoying, and that perhaps I would sleep in the hut.

"It will be better here," he said. "Spread a little straw on the bunk, put this old sheepskin coat under your head, and then cover yourself with a blanket. I'll warrant that you'll sleep like a babe in a cradle. It'll be a little more pleasant with two of us here."

After fixing up an improvised bed on the bunk near the wall, I came out of the hut and sat down on a bench alongside the old man, where we each lit a *makhorka* cigarette. Zuchok curled up beside us.

It was a warm night in August. The sky was full of twinkling stars, and the grain fields were alive with the chirping of the crickets and the call of the quails. From time to time the croak of herons could be heard as they flew high in the sky on their way to a fishing expedition in the Dnieper River.

I decided to confess everything to the old man, for he was not the kind of person who would inform on me. I started out by telling him about my father whose property was also liquidated in 1930, but who was murdered by the Communists at the age of seventy-three. I told him about my life in Kiev, in prison, in Siberia; and how I finally landed at the MTS. Having every reason to believe that the NKVD would now be looking for me, I avoided sleeping at home, and that was why I had come to the hut at this time of the night. I told him that I would rise early in order to create the impression that I had arrived early.

"Yes, yes, my son," replied the old man, after he had silently listened to my story. "I see that you also have tasted the bitter cup of sorrow. I know how you feel. It is ten years now since I heard from my son, my daughter-in-law, and my grandson in Siberia; so I have concluded that they must be dead. Why, oh why, does the Lord not punish these snakes in Moscow who murder innocent people? In order to have a little peace before my death I keep strictly silent about these matters. When I do speak it is mostly to myself or to Zuchok as we make the rounds of these fields. I see a good deal of what goes on in this bitter world, but I can do nothing but cry a little. It won't be long now until I'll be gone. But you still have a long life before you. Maybe sometime you will be able to tell your children about our new serfdom. You needn't fear me; I won't tell anyone. And when you are forced to hide out, I'll bring you a piece of bread from time to time. You will be safe here at night, for Zuchok will be able to tell at once if anybody is coming. I'm near this hut most of the time, although every once in a while I have to take a look at the grain shed."

We sat thus until midnight. He asked many questions concerning Siberia, and sometimes he would sigh heavily.

Then he got up, saying, "I think you had better retire now as it is rather late. I am going on my rounds, but I shall soon come back again. Sleep tight. Zuchok will be on the watch. I won't forget to wake you up early."

The warmth in his voice reminded me of my own father.

And so for four successive nights I slept out in the field. I would first eat supper, and then, when night began to fall, I would return by a roundabout way to the hut.

"It looks as if that brunette must have turned your head to keep you beating that path to her doorstep. Who is it that keeps you out so much at night?" asked my landlady.

"Perhaps there'll be a wedding celebration in our house soon," my landlord added with a smile.

I passed it off lightly, telling them that I had been visiting a neighbouring farmstead. I did not want to share my secret with them. Not that I distrusted them at all, but because I had to exercise extreme caution — a virtue that I had acquired by bitter experience.

Two days after my first talk with the MTS director, we met again and he greeted me cordially. He asked me how my work was getting on, and how everything was. I told him that things were running along smoothly.

"Don't mention our last conversation to anyone," he cautioned. "I spoke to nobody about it."

So, I had not been mistaken in my feeling that this man wanted to warn me of danger. Every night when I went home I proceeded cautiously as I neared the house in order to observe whether anybody might be waiting for me. And during the day, on my tractor, I was extremely uneasy. I was on the watch for any strangers approaching.

At the hut, with Grandpa and the dog on guard, things seemed a little more peaceful. Sometimes Zuchok would run out to the road barking and the old man would come out of the hut to see what the matter was, while I retired into the wheat field where I could observe the situation with greater safety. But such incidents were rare, as the steppe at night was almost devoid of travellers. Only rarely would some passerby come to the hut to enquire about the direction of the village.

One evening after midnight the *kolkhoz* chief came with the foreman to see whether there had been any grain thefts. When the old man woke me up I hid myself until they went away. But in spite of being well guarded, I kept having troubled dreams. Grandpa told me I often yelled and groaned in my sleep. Forebodings of danger depressed me.

Several nights after I started sleeping in the field we heard the far-off sounds of cannon thunder. We listened intently in the quiet of the night. Or was it bombs dropped by the aeroplanes? Up till now the Information Bureau had told only of battles in the Bila Tserkva vicinity, but this sounded much closer. Whatever it was, I decided that it would be best in a couple of days to secure a two-day leave of absence from the director, to go to N. I would hide out somewhere in the locality, and never appear among these people again. They would think that I had been held at N., and so would not look for me here.

I spoke of my intention to no one but Grandpa, and he promised to feed me if I came to him at night.

The next day, the 12th of August, 1941, I returned to the field in the evening. The sky was darkened with clouds, and it soon began to rain. Grandpa and I entered the hut, talking in whispers. We talked of many things, and Zuchok dozed somewhere on the straw under the hut. It had begun to rain heavily, and the patter of the rain drops on the roof made us all sleepy.

I continued with my story, but my listener was now snoring slightly. I spoke to him but he did not reply. It was around midnight, and as I listened to the monotonous tip-tap of the rain I slipped into a deep slumber.

Suddenly someone pulled me by the hand. I woke up immediately and sat up on the bunk.

"What's the matter?" I asked.

But no one answered. I could barely make out the outline of the open door and the shadow of someone leaving the hut. Zuchok was by the door, barking furiously. I heard some horses snorting. The rain was coming down in torrents.

Having noted all this quickly, I rose hurriedly and put on my running shoes, intending to rush out of the hut and hide somewhere. But I saw at once that this was impossible, for near the door could be seen the silhouettes of some people speaking with Grandpa. I withdrew to the bunk and lay down with my face towards the door, covering myself with a blanket. I couldn't hide under the bunk for it was packed with chests filled with instruments and machine supply parts.

Holding my breath I tried to catch some of the conversation, but it was drowned out by the rain and the barking of Zuchok. The old man chased him away but couldn't quieten him.

"Is Pavlenko sleeping here?" I heard someone ask, and it seemed to be the voice of the *komsomol* secretary.

I could not make out what Grandpa answered, but I now knew that they had come for me!

"Why are you loafing around here in the hut?" he asked the old man. "Go back to the granary."

Grandpa evidently obeyed, for Zuchok's barking became less and less audible. A couple of people were mumbling near the door, but they spoke in such low tones that I couldn't make out what they were saying. I saw two dim silhouettes within the contours of the door.

After a while one of the persons entered the hut, halting near the door to light a match. I put up a pretence of sound sleep by snoring loudly, although I watched the secretary through my nearly closed eyes. Without turning around he beckoned to his partner, and another man quietly entered the hut. By the last flicker of the burning match I recognized an NKVD cap, and I noticed that both of them had rifles.

I kept up the pretence of snoring with evenly divided pauses, so that I could listen in on their conversation. After closing the door, they apparently sat down and I heard them talking quietly to each other.

I listened intently, meanwhile snoring rhythmically, but I was unable to catch what they were saying, for the rain still kept falling noisily upon the roof. I could hear the pawing and snorting of the horses outside. Two words, *do utra* or "until tomorrow," reached my ears quite plainly. I decided that they would not bother me until the dawn. Perhaps they were influenced by the darkness and the rain.

My brain was now seething, and I felt as if I were electrified. With lightning-like rapidity the events of my life in prison, and in Siberia passed before me like a hideous dream.

Somewhere in the distance could be heard the noise of approaching bombers. I felt so depressed that I would not have cared if a bomb had exploded on our hut. Death was more welcome than the kind of life I had suffered in the past and which now seemed like a horrible nightmare. It was the second time in my experience when I would not have run away from sudden death.

CHAPTER 24

I Make My Escape

IMMEDIATELY AFTERWARDS my mind was feverishly seeking a way out. I recalled the cellar under the former chapel of the Lukianiwska prison in Kiev and the stories of Hulakov about the cellar of death in the NKVD garage on Rosa Luxembourg Street. There was only one conclusion. Either I was to act like a man or be lost. It was easier to die from a bullet on an open field than in a damp, blood-spattered cellar.

I remembered how my mother used to pray for me. Maybe the power of that prayer would save me now, as it seemed to have done more than once before. Strangely enough the very thought of it comforted me. I seemed to have regained control over my nerves, and a new-found strength and resolution surged through me.

I continued snoring a few more minutes without listening to the conversation, but I was thinking over the details of a plan of escape. Those few minutes seemed like hours.

Finally I yawned loudly, as if I were just awakening

out of a deep sleep. Then I stretched out on the bunk. The guards quieted down, listening intently. I coughed out loud, and then let my legs slide off the bed. I rustled a paper in my hands and leisurely rolled a cigarette in the dark, although my hands were trembling violently. Having rolled my cigarette, I slammed the tobacco box purposely down on the bench by the bunk.

There was dead silence by the door. I got up on my feet, and lighted a match. Assuming a manner of natural surprise, I pretended to notice for the first time that there were people in the hut. I wanted to create the impression of complete composure. Holding the match out before me, without moving from where I stood, and assuming a completely indifferent and sleepy tone of voice, I said, "Oh! I see the rain has also driven you here. It will likely pour till morning."

In answer the secretary gruffly muttered that they were soaked to the skin.

"Whose fault is it that you wander over the field at a time like this?" I said. "With those rifles it seems you've been hunting for diversionists."

I lit my cigarette, puffed on it a few times, and then lit another match, as if to avoid stumbling over the bench. I made for the door.

"Where are you going?" the secretary asked angrily.

"Into a crevice," I said. "Who would want to go out in such a rain?"

Holding the rifle in one hand, and the door-knob in the other, the secretary opened the door a little but kept his hold on the knob. The other fellow was sitting on the bench opposite the door, holding on to his rifle with both hands. All these details photographed themselves on my mind.

Without waiting another second, I set myself for a final plunge, and then hit the door with every ounce of strength in me. This move took the secretary by surprise, for I heard the hard thump of his body and the metallic clatter of his rifle as they both fell to the floor. Even if he had expected it, he would not have been able to stop me, so furious was the impact, to which desperation added strength. I landed on all fours in a pool of water; but I got up quickly, swerved to the side, and then made off into the wheat field.

I heard shouts of "Halt, halt!" behind me, and then a few shots. One bullet whizzed perilously close to me, but I ran on as fast as I could. For several minutes I heard nothing behind me. Perhaps they were untying their horses. I kept on running.

For a while all was quiet. Then there were some rifle shots and the sound of hoof beats. I kept on plunging through the wheat, and when the beat of horses' hoofs became more distinct, I covered the last lap to a Cossack mound. I had then run about a quarter of a mile.

My breath was spent. My heart-beats seemed to be bursting my throat. My tongue was a dry stick. I was rain-soaked and drenched. Finally I could run no farther, and I flopped down on the ground in the wheat field, crossing myself meanwhile.

The hoof-beats were now very close. There were two more shots, and I could even hear the horses breathing. As I flattened myself on the ground I thought of my mother's prayer. At that moment one of the riders raced by about fifteen or twenty paces from me. It seemed to me that his horse had galloped right over my head. I remained still as death. The other horseman galloped after him, and both kept on going, shooting off their rifles from time to time. As they got farther and farther away my heart began to beat quietly again. I sucked the rain water out of a handful of wheat grains to wet my parched tongue. After waiting a few minutes until the hoof-beats could no longer be heard, I got up and proceeded as quietly as I could to a nearby ravine. The riders might return and it was dangerous to remain in the field any longer.

I heard a few more shots, and then nothing but the splashing of the raindrops on the ground. From time to time I stopped to listen. There was no other sound except that somewhere in the distance I could hear the faint barking of Zuchok. Perhaps they had returned to see whether I was hiding in the grain shed. With great faith in my mother's prayer, which had apparently once more saved me, I crossed myself again.

Having become used to the dark, I soon found a path which I followed towards the hiding-place I had previously mentioned to Anatoli. I stepped cautiously so as not to trample down the clover, parted the branches of the bush, and slid down into the hole. The water gurgled under me as it washed around my shoes. From overhead it was trickling down my neck and face. The bush did not protect me very much.

There wasn't a dry stitch on me. The night was cool and I began to shiver. My teeth chattered so that if my pursuers had been near they would have heard me.

I could have gone to some strawstack not too far away, but I did not want to leave any trail; and to remain there would not have been safe, for a stack would have been a logical place to search for me. There was no use in going back to grandpa for the same reason. I tried to make the best of the situation by standing up and stamping in the muddy water.

Shortly after dawn the rain ceased. The eastern sky began to grow light, and the steppe came to life again with the chirping of the birds.

Without crawling out of my hole, I quickly undressed, wrung out my clothing, and then dressed again. After I poured the water out of my shoes, I began to feel a little better. I even dozed a little. When the sun finally rose, I warmed up somewhat; but I did not dare to leave my hide-out. Any footprints that I had made before I came to the hole must have been obliterated completely by the rain and so I could not have been followed even by a dog. That is what I counted on.

Although it was extremely unpleasant and uncomfortable in my cramped and soggy quarters, I decided to stick it out until the search abated, or at least until the following evening. Cautiously parting the branches of the bush,

I poked my head out to take a look around. There were no people out on the steppe. The grain was still quite damp, and nobody would come out into the fields to work until it had dried somewhat.

Around eight or nine o'clock I noticed four figures near the distant hut. I could only see their heads and shoulders, as the rest of their bodies were hidden by the shoulder of a ravine. I watched them carefully but could not recognize them at that distance. After a few minutes two of them took leave and came along the road in the direction of the ravine. I could follow their course at first, but they soon disappeared beyond a bend in the road. They appeared again at the point where the road led down into the ravine, after which they turned off from the road onto a path which traversed the whole length of the ravine past my hide-out. I slid farther down in my hole, but left a large enough opening to keep them in sight. They were coming nearer and nearer and now I was able to recognize the foreman. I noticed a blue cap on the head of the other man. This evidently was the fellow who had pursued me. The foreman carried a carbine on his shoulder, with the barrel pointing downwards. His companion wore a pistol at his side.

I sat down deeper in my hole, holding my breath. Although my hide-out was very close to the path, it could not readily be discovered as all that could be seen was a small bush among the clover, which covered the opening. My own discovery of this hide-out, as I stated previously, was a mere accident.

Now, when death was so near to me, so close that the voices of my would-be killers were very distinct, I prayed and I thought of my mother's prayer. Without moving so much as a finger, I listened. Were they actually deviating towards me from the path or not? If they discovered me I had determined to jump out and run for it. I would not have gotten away but I would have tried.

The voices died away, and I again raised my head. They were going in the direction of the strawstack and the grove of trees, and they soon disappeared from view behind a bend. Again I looked around cautiously without thrusting my head through the bush. Around the hut more people were now milling about, but I could not recognize any of them.

I concentrated my whole attention on the bend in the path behind which my pursuers were now hidden. About two hours later the two men appeared at the bend again. I hardly breathed while I listened to their footsteps and voices, as they came nearer and nearer and finally passed. A great desire to sneeze came over me, as I was catching cold. I grabbed the front of my shirt and held it tightly against my mouth and nose, bending my head down to my knees. Nothing happened. Perhaps I was fated to live a little longer.

I longed for a smoke, but I had left the tobacco box in the hut. I was hungry too. I smothered these impossible hopes. There was no alternative but to sit and wait until nightfall, as I did not dare to come out and warm myself in the sun.

During the day several people passed my cave along the path. I peered at them cautiously, but there was no occasion for fear, as they were all ordinary unarmed peasants. In the evening one of them came along with his dog, but the dog did not even look in my direction. At nightfall, I straightened up to my full height, for my whole body had become numb.

Now I debated whether I should visit Grandpa. I was afraid of a trap, however, for this was a time when they might be expecting me to go there. I wanted to smoke very badly and also to eat. Even a crust of bread would have been wonderful but I finally decided to stick it out for another day and let my pursuers think that I had departed from the district.

I thought that I might be able to make a cigarette from leaves. I plucked some dry leaves off the bush that had shielded me, and then searched for some paper. I found a half dry piece of newspaper in my pocket. Straightening it out carefully so that it would not fall apart, I placed it under my shirt against my chest to dry it out. I dried my matches in the same manner. In half an hour I slumped down in my hole to enjoy a few puffs from my blackberry leaf cigarette.

It was a warm night in August. After yesterday's downpour the quails whistled and the crickets chirped more loudly, as if they were making up for lost time. Somewhere around ten o'clock the distant boom of cannon fire could be heard distinctly. High up in the heavens could be seen flying formations of bombers. I tried to fall asleep leaning against the earth walls of my hide-out, but it was still too damp and cold. I then thought of bringing in some straw. The strawstack was not far away. After listening intently for any suspicious noises, I crawled out of my hide-out and set out for the straw, being careful not to disturb the clover too much. All the way to the stack I kept my ears tuned for any unusual noises or sounds. Everything was quiet, and nobody was around. But before I reached the stack I sat down in the clover, listening for any noises at the strawstack, as there might be a trap. Everything was quiet. To prevent strewing the straw along the path, I took my shirt off and filled it full, taking it back to the hole in a roundabout way. It was now warmer in the cave, and I at last fell asleep, for I was dead tired.

In my slumber it seemed as if some one were coughing. I was wide awake at once. There was another cough. I remained still so as not to rustle the straw. Someone called me by my name. The call was repeated. It sounded like the voice of Anatoli. I got up carefully and looked out. I could see the silhouette of a person against the night sky, standing not far from me on the path. I kept quiet until he called me by name again. I had no more doubts. It was Anatoli.

In answer I told him to remain on the path until I came out to him. I semi-circled around to him in order not to leave any direct trail; but when I finally reached him we embraced as though we were blood-brothers. He had brought me some bread, a small piece of pork fat, a bottle of milk, some *makhorka*, and a small flask of vodka. Never in my life had I ever received so precious a gift.

We went farther away to the opposite slope of the ravine and sat down. I at once attacked the food, and he did the talking.

"Your landlady told me that they had come to get you late at night. Not finding you there they made inquiries. She told them that you had gone to a party. They looked for you everywhere. The foreman remained in the room along with a *komsomolist*, waiting until dawn. But the NKVD man and the secretary rode off into the field on horseback. Grandpa told me so. They questioned him also, but he said that he did not know anything. This morning at dawn they came to me asking whether I knew where you were. They searched everywhere. They told me to inform the foreman if I found out anything about you. Inform them, indeed!

"They were searching for you all over the steppe today, questioning people here and there. But I guessed at once that you were here. I would like to invite you to my place, but I think it would be better to wait, as they might call upon me again. Tomorrow I shall bring you something more to eat."

Thanking him, I asked him if he could bring me some clothing as it was chilly at night. That very same night he brought me a cap and a jacket. I now felt like a king. Settling down in my hole, warmed by the vodka and the jacket, I fell into a deep sleep and did not wake up till noon of the next day.

The next day passed quietly. Some people passed by me on their way to work in the fields, but they were harmless.

The next night Anatoli brought me more food and thus I had no need of visiting Grandpa. I asked my friend to send him my best regards, as I knew the old man was anxious about me. Anatoli told me that the Germans were now very close, and that local Communists were preparing for flight. The MTS had already been given orders to plough under the sugar beet crop. Peter had driven in that day with a five-unit gang plough, but soon the tractor babbit bearing wore out because he "forgot" to put in oil, and so the beets were still growing. The MTS director publicly scolded him, claiming that this was sabotage, but he did not punish him. Later on he was told to take the tractor to the repair shop and that was all there was to it.

"Tomorrow I shall take you to my place. I have prepared a good hide-out for you in the attic, where at least you'll be able to lie down and sleep. I don't think they'll have time to look for you anymore."

The following night Anatoli led me across the fields and gardens to his home and hid me in the attic behind some old window frames and straw sheaves. Stretching out on the straw and under a warm quilt I fell into a profound sleep from which I did not waken until evening.

I remained in this new hide-out another five days. By now sounds of the cannon shots had become more audible. Anatoli told me that the local Communists were loading wagons with all kinds of provisions from the *kolkhoz* storehouse; that they were slaughtering pigs and making preparations for sudden flight.

"I think," he said, "that the MTS director is just pretending that he wants to flee. If you ask me, I think he intends to remain behind. It is rumoured that he has instructions to destroy everything at the last moment, all the machinery and stacks of grain. It is hardly likely that he will do this. No one is working on the fields any more, and the machinery is just lying around idle. Only yesterday two 'comrades' came in an auto to poison all the grain in the granaries. The same thing was done to piles and piles of grain at the station."

On the sixth day of my stay upstairs, Anatoli swiftly climbed the ladder.

"Come down quickly. The German tanks are here!"

We all ran outside. Some distance away in long line formation many tanks marked with black and white crosses were proceeding forward through the stubble. Preceding the tanks were a couple of dozen motorcyclists carrying machine-guns. That day they occupied the town of N. without any opposition.

In the local NKVD cellar 148 bodies were found. All had had their hands tied behind their backs, and had been shot in the nape of the neck. The 149th escaped this fate through the influence of a mother's prayers.

The arrival of the Germans meant, for me, escape from the terror of the Russian NKVD. It was the first step on the long, rough road to freedom which brought me eventually to Canada — the great wide land where a man can live and work and speak freely, without fear and in fellowship with his fellow-men.

Somewhere, far behind the Iron Curtain, in places unknown, are the graves of my mother, my father and my sister. There, also, are the countless graves of my countrymen who died in the struggle with Muscovite tyranny.

Their spirit still lives on today. It cannot be shackled and shot in the nape of the neck. One day it will triumph and my enslaved Ukraine will join the family of freedom-loving nations.

Glossary

aul, mountain village in Georgia

balanda, slops

bytovyky, prisoner guilty of a criminal, as opposed to a political, offence

Black Crow, a closed police van or Black Maria

kartser, a dungeon-cell for solitary confinement

kolkhoz, a collective farm, as organized by the Soviet State

kollegiya, a court

makhorka, poor quality tobacco

MTS, Machine Tractor Station

Narkom, a word coined by syllabification from *Narodny Komisar*, i.e. "Peoples' Commissar," the minister in charge of a government department. In 1943, the term was replaced by "Minister"

Narkomat, coined similarly from *Narodny Komisariat* or "People's Commissariat," a government department. In 1945, the term was replaced by "Ministerium"

Narzam, Georgian Mineral Water

NKVD, the Narodny Komisariat Vnutrennikh Dyel, or "People's Commissariat for Internal Affairs," i.e. the political ministry, earlier known as the Cheka and the OGPU, and since 1943 as the MVD

NZP, Ne Zakonnoe Prozivanie, illegal residence

OSO, a special NKVD court which tries the accused in absentia and in secret

Radhosp, State Farm

seksot, coined by syllabification from *sekretny sotrudnik*, a "secret collaborator" or police informer

SWU, Soyuz Wyzvolennja Ukraying or "Union for the Freedom of the Ukraine"

taiga, the subarctic wilderness of spruce, pine and cedar forest in Siberia

Voyenkomat, Voyenny Komisariat or "Army Office"